A BRIEF FANTASY HISTORY

OF A HIMALAYAN

A Brief
Fantasy History

OF A HIMALAYAN

Autobiographical Reflections

THINLEY NORBU

SHAMBHALA
Boston & London
2014

SHAMBHALA PUBLICATIONS, INC.
Horticultural Hall
300 Massachusetts Avenue
Boston, Massachusetts 02115
www.shambhala.com

9 8 7 6 5 4 3 2 1

First Edition
Printed in the United States of America

♾ This edition is printed on acid-free paper that meets
the American National Standards Institute z39.48 Standard.
♻ Shambhala Publications makes every effort to print on recycled paper.
For more information please visit www.shambhala.com.

Distributed in the United States by Penguin Random House LLC
and in Canada by Random House of Canada Ltd

Designed by Lora Zorian

LIBRARY OF CONGRESS CATALOGING-IN-PUBLICATION DATA

Thinley Norbu, author.
A brief fantasy history of a Himalayan:
autobiographical reflections / Thinley Norbu.
pages   cm
ISBN 978-1-61180-205-4 (hardback)
1. Thinley Norbu. 2. Buddhist monks—Biography. I. Title.
BQ990.H55T55 2014
294.3'923092—dc23
[B]
2013048264

NOTE TO THE READER

*I*N HIS BOOK *The Small Golden Key,* Kyabje Thinley Norbu Rinpoche related: "I wrote *A Brief Fantasy History of a Himalayan* in the countryside of New York in the springtime amid swaying weeping willow trees because some of my loving American friends requested me to tell my life history. They helped me through their fanatical, positive hallucination phenomena toward me and my speech which is like brass, but which they saw like pure gold and tried to make as an ornament for the Buddha's teaching."

The writing was begun in 1980, but Rinpoche did not want to publish it until making additions about his later years. Although a few inserts were added in the 1990s, Rinpoche did not get to finish this book as he had wished; however, he continued writing other books that he considered to be more important for the benefit of others. Rinpoche was never concerned about anything to do with himself. Yet this brief book is actually very important for others, because it gives some details of Rinpoche's life never recounted anywhere else, and especially because it allows us a glimpse of the inconceivable selfless nature of this buddha who appeared in the world only for others, quietly teaching and showing through his extraordinary kindness and his completely pure, profound example how to practice in a simple way and how to open to wisdom. Like everything written by Rinpoche, it is a guide to enlightenment.

In this new edition, for the convenience of interested readers we have added a section in the back giving the Tibetan, English, or Sanskrit equivalents for selected names, titles, and terms.

A BRIEF FANTASY HISTORY
OF A HIMALAYAN

Everything is fantasy created by illusory mind
Everything is fantasy contained within illusory mind
The eternalist view is fantasy to the nihilist
The nihilist view is fantasy to the eternalist
Both views are fantasy to the Buddhist
The past is fantasy since we can't see it now
The future is fantasy since we can't use it now
The present is fantasy since we can't find it now
If everything is fantasy, this history is also fantasy
If everything is true, this history is also true
So, may you, Lord Buddha, most sublime fantasy
Bless this short fantasy history
Which my fantasy friends asked me to write
For the benefit of all sentient being fantasizers

$\mathcal{M}$Y FATHER IS THE EMANATION OF Blood-Drinking Islander, Subduer of Evil. In sublime histories, Blood-Drinking Islander is described as very wrathful, radiant, and splendid, with a fierce white beard and piercing eyes. He wore spiral conch shell earrings and dressed in the ancient, snow mountain great yogi's style. His hair was tied up at the top of his head in a knot, symbolic of abiding in the great samadhi of Mahasandhi, with the rest loose and uncontrived by worldly custom; his clothes were white and uncontrived by other colors; and his unending natural mind was self-liberated and uncontrived by dualistic thoughts. He received teachings on the alphabet and language from beings with ordinary human form visible to general perception, but mostly he received wisdom transmissions from sublime beings through his personal pure perception of visions invisible to others. He kept a sky-iron kilaya symbolic of the four great wish-fulfillments, and tucked in his sash a sword symbolic of the wisdom weapon, and sometimes, when exorcising possessed beings, he would hit them with a ferocious strike of the back of the sword. Everyone was terrified of his fierce nature. He was always subduing demon-minded beings through his wrathful compassion.

Before his death he said to his disciples, "Now it is the unlucky degenerate age and there will be war with the enemies of Buddhism, so we should go to the Hidden Land of Lotus Ornament blessed by Padmasambhava's sunlight feet. You go before me. I am an old man and I will follow slowly after you." Then many disciples left their country for the Hidden Land of Lotus Ornament, but before most of them reached their destination, he had passed into his next emanation form.

My father's name is Fearless Wisdom Vajra. He was born east of the Himalayas in the Hidden Land of Lotus Ornament, as his previous incarnation had predicted. His mother's family came from Dragonland. When he was young, because of his graceful, androgynous appearance, it was

Dudjom Lingpa (Blood-Drinking Islander, Subduer of Evil).

sometimes difficult for strangers to recognize whether he was a man or a woman. He had long hair that was sometimes left loose and sometimes plaited, and he wore clothes in the Snowland ordinary yogi's style, except during special ceremonies when he dressed according to the Vajrayana custom. He had many sublime teachers, including Empowered Changeless True Meaning, his previous incarnation's disciple, who recognized him in this next incarnation. Extraordinarily gifted, he has organized many texts of treasure holders, especially those of his previous incarnation. From the time he was a teenager, profound hymns and songs came to him naturally that awakened readers like the self-sounding of Dharmata. The fingers of old intellectual scholars could not write meaningfully in this way even with their pens aimed in tight concentration just like seagulls waiting at the

Kyabje Dudjom Rinpoche (Fearless Wisdom Vajra).

shore for fish who rarely come. He has written many shastras and given initiations and tantric teachings up to the Great Perfection. His disciples include a great variety of scholars, monks, nuns, laypeople, yogis, yoginis, and lamas, and cannot be numbered. Everyone is spoiled by his gentle nature, and he is always blessing fortunate beings through peaceful compassion and subduing demon-minded beings through exposing their dormant evil qualities. He has no certain, definite ideas, so he just echoes other beings' demands and desires. He has no self-grasping judgment, so many self-seeking beings often misuse him as capital for their own self-promotion, just as there are many beings surrounding the Gandhola of Bodh Gaya and the Stupa of Boudhanath who do not have even one iota of faith, but are relying on these stupas to do their business.

My mother's name is Turquoise Lamp of Firm Life. She was born west of the Himalayas near the Great Ocean River of Offering and came from a renowned noble family named Family Branch of Front-Facing Fortress. During her youth in Snowland, it was the custom for aristocrats to marry aristocrats, but she was only interested in marrying a Buddhist teacher. She has great faith in many sublime beings including Buddha, Padmasambhava, Tara, and her root guru, Noble Priestess Yogini of Phenomena Space, who was an emanation of a sublime-crazy yogini named Sole Mother Lamp of Labchi, whose teacher, a wisdom saint named Sole Holy Buddha Father, said, "One night I heart-whispered three words and she was liberated."

My mother often tells wonderful tales and sad histories of awesome Bodhisattvas and saints. Her nature is unpossessive and eccentric, detached and untouchable. She is always worshiping, praying, and making offerings. She especially likes to make offerings with fresh water, and wherever she stays, she is always bringing water, filling empty pots with water, and scattering water everywhere. When it rains, even if she is only half dressed, she runs outside, holding cups to the sky to collect water for offerings. She is so much in love with water, she seems like the emanation of Mamaki.

She prefers candles to electricity, and her house looks like a chicken coop because the floor is covered with thousands of drops of wax. Sometimes in the autumn, she can be seen climbing the fruit trees to pick fruit for offerings from her pure intention before they have dropped on the land. She avoids the people left to take care of her, saying that they

With Mayum Tseten Yudron-la (Turquoise Lamp of Firm Life), mother, and Phende Norbu Rinpoche (Jewel of Beneficial Well-Being), brother, in Sikkim.

*Semo Dechen Yudron-la
(Turquoise Radiance of Great Bliss), sister.*

With Chökyi Nyima Rinpoche (Sun of Dharma), brother (left), in Tibet.

Semo Pema Yudron-la
(Lotus of Turquoise Light), sister.

prevent her from being free, and prefers to be looked after by careless youngsters because they let her do what she wishes. She likes to cook by herself, and has often burned her clothes when she took the pots off the stove with her sleeves and skirt. When we scold her and say, "This is not according to correct worldly custom," or "This is not according to correct Dharma custom," she answers, "There is no meaning to correct worldly custom, so how can I act according to it? There is no substance to correct Dharma custom, so how can I act according to it?"

Many ordinary people think my mother is crazy and insult her, and many sublime beings say she is truly a wisdom sky-goer and praise her. She always loves, praises, and prays for each of her children from her heart. She didn't know how to teach us to support ourselves in a worldly way; she only tried to lead us to Dharma.

I was born in the Land of the Gods, between east and west, in the center, near the Temple of Miraculous Goat-Earth Phenomena. My family, like the Seven Northern Stars, had seven children. My elder sister's name is Turquoise Radiance of Great Bliss. She has a warm and open nature with everyone. My name is Jewel of Activity. I am the oldest son. Following me, there is a brother named Sun of Dharma whose nature is honest, pure, clean, angry, and noble. My next sister is named Lotus of Turquoise Light. She looked like an angel princess just descending from heaven. I thought that if the drought of human aging did not exist, she would always be every hero's heart-thief. My brother, named Jewel of Beneficial Well-Being, is very generous, kind, humble, and unconcerned about doing anything himself for this ordinary life, which is actually of no concern, but causes those who love him to worry. My youngest brother, named Indestructible Noble Glory, was very fresh and brave with a natural mind. In his youth he was murdered by the savage Red Guard for his heroic resistance. My youngest sister, named Melodious Long Life, had a very good sense of humor and was always laughing. But as samsara's words always entice beings, she was lured by her name and passed away when she was very young.

As Buddha Shakyamuni said, "By its nature, all worldly gathering has its end in separation," and so I was separated from my family when I was eight years old. At that time I went to study the Holy Dharma of Snowland at the monastery of the Sublime Island of Ripening Liberation under the direction of Jewel of the Occurrence of All Qualities, and stayed there until I was seventeen years old, studying language, rituals, and philosophy. The head of the monastery was named Younger Jewel of Conquering Speech of Dharma's Renown. His morality was as precious to him as his own eyes, and his constant discipline seemed to come directly from the most serene face of Buddha Shakyamuni. One of my teachers was a wise and great doctor named Great Bliss Dharma Holder of the Vajra. He healed countless patients impartially like a Bodhisattva. Wherever he went, the smell of natural medicine accompanied him, like a messenger from the Medicine Buddha pureland. Another one of my teachers, named Ocean of Intelligence, taught language, rituals, Vinaya vows, bodhichitta teachings, and Vajrayana samaya. With his magnificent form and thick black beard, he seemed like a trainer sent from a powerful wisdom king to subdue my wild elephant mind with his skillful hook.

In those days, great ceremonies with dances were performed in the monastery every year. My dancing teacher's name was All-Loving Display, and I learned a few of these Dharma dances from him. I danced in the Crow Sword Dance, which was performed to analyze and distinguish between black demon and white deity. In Accepting the Offering, which was a group dance, I was one of the two who made the offerings. In the Command of the Lion's Roar, one of the dances of the Eight Manifestations of Padmasambhava, my role symbolized the blazing emanations of the lion's roar. All of these dances were very fast and in the wrathful style. I also danced the very slow and tranquil Five-Dakini Dance in a most beautiful ancient silk brocade costume with many bone and ivory jewel ornaments, beating the drum and singing praise to Padmasambhava's indestructible wisdom body, unobstructed wisdom speech, undeluded wisdom heart, immeasurable wisdom qualities, and effortless wisdom activities.

I became a little bit famous among the students as a dancer, and after dancing, when I entered the costume room, many monks would scatter rejoicing flowers of appreciation. When I saw my father, he would ask me to dance and I would dance for his entertainment.

In general, life in the monastery was very ascetic. The food and accommodations were simple, and because of the naughty nature of young boys, from time to time we were beaten as a substitute for candy. I stayed in the monastery for nine years, and during that time I saw my parents only three times.

When I was thirteen years old, I heard one of my teachers whispering with his friends that my parents had separated, but I didn't understand clearly what he meant. When I was seventeen years old and went to visit my parents in the center of Snowland, I still had the habit of seeing them together, but when I arrived at my father's house, I couldn't find my mother because they had separate homes. For a moment, I felt as if I had lost my precious heart. Soon my mother sent for me, and I went to see her with my brothers and sisters who were staying at home, and from then on, we went back and forth between our parents' houses.

At that time, my energy had become so constricted and my elements were under so much pressure from many years of pretending to be disciplined in the monastery that I exploded like a volcano. I became wild, riding horses, swimming in the river, arguing with young boys, and playing with my brothers and sisters. After a while, when my father asked me to return again to the monastery, I said, "No! I would rather jump in the river and die."

"If you don't want to return to the Sublime Island of Ripening Liberation, then you must go to the famous Glorious Lion Great Perfection Monastery in the East," he said. But again I replied that I would rather jump in the river and die.

Finally, he didn't send me to either monastery and took me instead to his residence named Superior Great Exaltation in the Forest Valley Land.

At that time, I didn't pay much attention to the country's aspect, but as I remember now, I think it was most beautiful. In Snowland, crops do not usually grow where the nomads live because the ground is too high, and nomads do not usually come where the farmers live because there is no place for their animals to graze, but in this land there were both animals and fields of grain. There were many fragrant juniper trees, and some of the dark green pine trees were so large and grand that groups of fifteen or twenty travelers could camp under the dry shelter of the branches of one tree on the fallen, soft, warm needles. In the autumn, parrots with red beaks and green feathers would chatter to each other noisily, eating the many different kinds of nuts and flying in groups from tree to tree in the open, light blue sky. You could easily see bears loping past the wild peach trees. There were different kinds of monkeys and many robins, quail, cuckoos, and wild pheasants, so tame in some places that they would eat without fear from the retreatants' hands.

There were many different rivers. Some churning rivers with white froth seemed to give warning; some rushing rivers with strong currents seemed to encourage; some flowing rivers with smooth waves seemed to give comfort; and some resting rivers with little ripples seemed to show new meditator's mind.

In the summer, the meadows were filled with so many bright-colored wildflowers that they seemed to teasingly paint us with their colors. In the autumn, the fields were filled with many delicious crops and the harvests were always abundant.

At that time, I had some other teachers in the Forest Valley Land. I learned grammar and practices from Tall Stone Emanation, and with Understanding of Phenomena I studied *Friend's Message* by Accomplished Lord Naga and *Entrance into Bodhisattva's Action* by Peaceful

God. From Vidyadhara of Oddiyana, the disciple of Great Scholar Victorious Speech, I listened to the reading of *The Seven Treasures* and *The Three Restings* by All-Knowing Vastly Profound Excellently Pervading, who is the emanation of Samantabhadra, and to the *Four Heart Drops* and *Vast Profound Heart Drop*. I listened to All-Knowing Loving Auspicious Majestic Accomplishment's reading and teaching of the king of tantras called *Essence of Secret Teachings,* and teachings of two of its commentaries, *Darkness of the Ten Directions Dispelled* by the Great Profound One, and *Ruler of the Secret Teachings' Wisdom Heart's Ornament* by the great translator Ocean of Glorious Dharma. From Able Teaching of Glorious Noble Activity, I took the initiation of *Four Heart Drops* by the Great Profound One, and listened to the reading of the *Treasury of Precious Qualities,* written by the wisdom holder Fearless Islander, and two of his commentaries on it, *Carriage of Two Truths* and *Carriage of Omniscience.* I listened to Enlightened Indestructible Freedom from Activity's reading of the *Song of the Wave of the Garuda's Wings* by Self-Liberated Six Senses.

Enlightened Indestructible Freedom from Activity's nature is very direct and he does not adapt to worldly people's manners. One time in Darjeeling, a rich merchant passed away suddenly from a heart attack. His widow requested many lamas to come to do the ritual of transference into pureland, which is done traditionally before a person takes his last breath. After he had taken his last breath, the corpse was still kept in the house since, according to Tibetan astrological tradition, the corpse cannot be removed from the house for the funeral until a certain day determined by his astrological chart. Sometimes that day comes soon after the last breath, but sometimes it is necessary to wait a while. The widow asked Enlightened Indestructible Freedom from Activity to come to her house to do the transference into pureland. After making prayers in front of the corpse, he asked the widow, "When are you going to remove the corpse from the house for the funeral?" Because it was summertime, and there was no place in Darjeeling to keep the body cold, the widow told him she was concerned that the corpse would begin to smell if she kept it in the house too long. With a worried voice, she said, "What to do?" Then Enlightened Indestructible Freedom from Activity answered, "Since you asked the astrologer, you have to do as he said. What is wrong if the corpse smells? You don't have to eat it and you don't have to sell it in the market."

From Great Excellent Oddiyana, I studied the stage of the transformation of ordinary appearances into pure deity appearance and the stage of characteristicless completion, and stayed in tantric samaya's inner Triple Gems retreat a few times under his guidance. His noble mind was unchangeable like a diamond; no impure substance could penetrate it. His stable mind was unshakable like Mount Meru; no coarse and turbulent wind could shake it. The consort of Great Excellent Oddiyana was named Glorious Destiny. Her smooth, elegant complexion was the color of milk, and her delicate body conquered my lust hermit's mind. Finally, she was the first to teach me how to sink my young swan's body into the blissful lake of desire.

When she guiltily blurted to Great Excellent Oddiyana about my continuous feelings, he asked me to stop because he was anxious that it would disturb my practice. But then when I tried to stop, he asked us to continue because he was anxious that other women would disturb my practice even more.

Glorious Destiny loved me deeply. In those days I had long hair, which she sometimes braided and sometimes let loose. When I washed, she always combed it and opened the part directly in the center. When I asked her, "Why don't you open the part on the side sometimes?" she answered, "It is symbolic of the direct path of open enlightenment, so it must be in the center. If you don't believe me, then look at the many statues and thangkas; they always open from the center."

Some people in my family had negative conceptions about us, but instead of being jealous, my teacher graciously gave his consort to me. Finally, when they departed in the direction of the land of the Manifestation of Rejoicing, they welcomed me to accompany them there or offered for her to remain with me if I should choose to stay behind. I decided to remain with my father.

I had a beautiful blue-gray and white dappled horse who had a long flowing mane. His name was Blue Turquoise Dragon, and he was my heart-fellow. I rode him to accompany them on the first day of their journey home. We slept in the autumn night under awning tents called noble white crane wings until the rooster from the neighboring village crowed at dawn.

Then Glorious Destiny said, "We are one family like the source of a mountain stream. If divided, it flows separated through the rugged valleys. Please, will you pray that we finally meet on the ocean's shore?"

Portrait of the youthful Kyabje Dudjom Rinpoche,
chosen by Thinley Norbu Rinpoche to hang in the
altar in his residence in Nepal.

And I answered, "Please keep the precious turquoise palace of your sky-mind unstained by clouds' shadows. Then, as the sun circles the five continents, I will return to you with warm, shining love." When it was time to leave, I offered my horse to them, knotting one end of a long white scarf to his forelock and putting the other end in her hand. We never met again in this life, but I am sure we will join as a result of our prayers according to relative truth and through our spiritual connection.

After that, I stayed with my father, taking initiations and teachings with his disciples, sometimes in small groups and sometimes in large groups. My father has countless disciples in the world, including in Tibet, Bhutan, Sikkim, and many other places. If, according to modern Dharma tradition, they made an advertisement with a photograph of disciples in order to materialize how many followers there are, it would be impossible to catch all these disciples. Among them were some students with very funny, spontaneous comedian's minds. For example, one precious, very simple disciple from Ladakh named Long Life came to my father's main residence in Kongpo and stayed there for many years, serving him by building temples and making gardens with stone. His nature was very noble and unsuspicious; he was never interested in worldly manners, but only in meditation. When my father was staying in India, near Durbindara, where his main residence was after the Chinese had occupied Tibet, Long Life would walk two miles back and forth to Durbindara each day to visit my father. In order to arrive at my father's house, he had to pass through an intersection where traffic police were stationed. One time, as he approached the intersection, he had to pee very badly. Since he never wore underwear, with his Tibetan clothes it was very easy for him to pee anytime. So he walked to the edge of the road and squatted there. While he was peeing, a policeman came and gently kicked him in his buttocks, saying, "You can't pee here in the intersection; you have to go to the bathroom to pee!" Long Life answered, "I couldn't find a bathroom, so can I pee in your mouth, please?" The policeman was upset and blew his whistle, and several more police came and took him to jail, where he stayed for three nights. When he was released, he asked them if he could stay longer because he was happy eating their delicious lentils and practicing in their jail. Later, he passed away from malaria.

He often cried with deep devotion, faith, and unbearable gratitude to my father, saying, "My tunnel vision was opened by my guru and now I can see sky."

My father had another student, a yogi named Plaited Hair who was an experienced practitioner of channels and airs. Through his energy, he could travel the distance in one day that it took others to travel in three days. He did not marry until late in life, keeping the sacred promise of channels and airs, according to which the practitioner is not supposed to lose sperm. He was returning to his district, Kullu, via Siliguri, and in order to wait for his late train, he lay down to sleep on the platform in a dark place beneath the overpass, like an ordinary passenger. His long plaited hair and his beardless face could easily be mistaken for a beautiful Tibetan woman's as he slept under his simple blanket, so, after midnight, a man tried to enter his bed. Plaited Hair, often playfully naughty, pretended to be a woman, making flirtatious feminine sounds from under his blanket and crying, "Please don't!" Then the man became more excited and forcefully entered his bed, climbing on him and pressing down on him with a big erection. Plaited

Hair was quite young, and having kept his sacred promise of not losing semen for many years, he also had a big erection. So he said, "OK!" and he hugged the man against him, pressing his pumped-up penis into the man's stomach. Extremely terrified, the man recognized that Plaited Hair was also a man and tried to get up. When Plaited Hair pulled him back, saying, "Don't leave me, let me have an orgasm!" he ran away as fast as he could. Immediately, other passengers came, inquiring, "What happened?" Also thinking that Plaited Hair was a woman, they warned her not to stay in the dark and scolded the escaped rapist. But Plaited Hair answered, "He is not a bad person, he is good. He had a big erection, as I do. Look at me!" Then he pulled up his Tibetan dress, showing his penis, and they all ran away.

At the age of eighteen, I started on my own life. For seven years, from the age of eighteen to twenty-five, I gathered experience. I spent some time sustaining a monastery that my father had given me when I was a young boy. There was a connection between the monastery and myself, because once, during my childhood when I was eight years old and my father was giving teachings there, I recovered from an illness after they made ritual long-life prayers for my health. The monastery was old, like an exhausted, haggard man, and there were about sixty peasant families connected to it. During those years, I had many problems through my inexperience.

I spent some time visiting, teaching, and traveling. One retreat place where I stayed was called Accepting Mountain of Great Bliss. Sometimes I silently exchanged fantasy phenomena with beautiful, fresh yoginis there.

Later, I went to central Snowland and visited with many great lamas: Indestructible Wisdom Teacher from Polo, Enlightened Indestructible Freedom from Activity Lama, and truly nonsectarian lama Gently Tuned Wisdom Intelligence of Phenomena, who embraced the teachings of all sects. I met him for the first time at Wish-Fulfilling Palace, the residence of an aristocratic officer, and later received essential precious teachings from him at Bodh Gaya. He said to me, "You can read countless texts and you can listen to countless teachings, but if you have determination in this unlucky degenerate age, it is best to

Wearing traditional fur hat and woolen robe
called a chuba, in Tibet, ca. 1950.

synthesize in your natural mind all the very precious teachings that can be found in the *Treasure of Space Phenomena*, by All-Knowing Vastly Profound Excellently Pervading."

One day I was invited with my father to have lunch at a merchant's house. Enlightened Indestructible Freedom from Activity and Gently Tuned Wisdom Intelligence of Phenomena were also there. They sat in a line on thrones and I sat in the corner near the door. I was dressed in the young Tibetan man's fashionable style. With conservative disapproval, Enlightened Indestructible Freedom from Activity introduced me to Gently Tuned Wisdom Intelligence of Phenomena and pointed out my style, not knowing that we had already met. But instead of scolding me, Wisdom Intelligence of Phenomena said, "Don't mind external custom. If you synthesize, the essence of all Buddha's teachings is intention. You must always try to increase good intention. That is all."

Later, I met all of these lamas again. I met Gently Tuned Wisdom Intelligence of Phenomena in Fruit Valley, where I received teachings on cutting through all substantial and insubstantial phenomena and

Kyabje Jamyang Khyentse Chökyi Lodrö Rinpoche
(Gently Tuned Wisdom Intelligence of Phenomena).

Young Rinpoche in Bhutan, ca. 1960, in a formal portrait wearing a plain chuba worn by lamas in Bhutan.

simultaneous passing, and I met Indestructible Wisdom Teacher from Polo, from whom I received teachings on Samantabhadra's Prayer of Basis, Path, and Result, and on the *Essence of Secret Teachings* and its commentaries. But it is not necessary to give an account here of the many different teachings, commentaries, sadhanas, and empowerments I received from different teachers. Rather than making a long list, creating prestige through my ego's boasting, it is better to try to practice what I was taught.

By that time, my father had moved to Supreme Shakya Sphere, my mother to Fruit Valley with my half sister, Holder of Wealth, and my other brothers and sisters were scattered, some together, some apart, throughout Snowland. I was left alone like a morning star.

Then one day, in the center of the Land of the Gods, I met my future wife's sister, Happy Long-Life Dharma, a very talkative and good-humored person with a powerful mind. She liked to ignore the orders of high-ranking official men, saying, "My fart is one hundred times more powerful than their command."

Following the ancient Snowland and Dragonland tradition in

which old-style parents, wishing a meaningful life for their children, try to provide for them a life-long loving companion with complementary spiritual qualities, she gave me a present and a letter from my future father-in-law inviting me to come to Dragonland to meet my future wife. So I accepted their invitation and accompanied Happy Long-Life Dharma and her retinue to Dragonland.

It was springtime and on horseback we crossed many fields with farmers working on them. On the first day, as the farmers opened their irrigation channels, streams of water began to flow toward me in the field. I thought it was very auspicious, and I offered this unexpected good omen to the Triple Gems. We traveled for a few days, and when we were nearly there, we found many yogis and yoginis waiting in the Dragonland style of welcome.

Some ritual offerings had been made in our honor. In general, rituals for purification and accumulation are expressed through the five-element goddesses. Sublime clay statues are made through the earth-element goddess, water purification offerings through the water-element goddess, fire and smoke offerings through the fire-element goddess, prayer and incense through the air-element goddess, and supreme samadhi siddhi through the space-element goddess.

In Dragonland's ancient auspicious tradition, they were burning sweet-smelling ferns and juniper leaves and lined the road in groups with baskets of red and white rice and fried maize piled high. They made a path of cut trees with prayer flags leading to an opening where they had spread carpets for us to rest. They arranged butter tea and silver-belted bamboo pots filled with wine and whiskey.

The leader of one group was called Smooth Melodious Lamp of Dharma. Later, she became my life's companion. She was born in the Upper Valley of Amusement between Padmasambhava's two sacred places in Dragonland, Lion's Fortress and Hidden Fern Valley. At that time, she was eighteen years old with a noble, fresh young body and glowing complexion. She was taller than the others and a little exotic-looking, dressed simply with a long red robe and sash.

I easily noticed that she was more enchanting than the others in the group, and I was excited, wondering who she was. I asked my friend who had accompanied me from Snowland, a student of my father-in-law's with a good sense of humor, "Who is that alluring and noble young girl?" He said, "Be patient. She will seduce you soon."

With Sangyum Jamyang Chödrön-la
(Smooth Melodious Lamp of Dharma), ca. 1956.

After tea, we left the group and went to my future father-in-law's house. His name was Exalted Instructor of Noble Destiny, and he was splendid like a noble sage from ancient times. When he was young, he spent years in Snowland and Buddha's Toe-Petal Blossom Land, serving many teachers, including his root guru and root guru's sons. He had faith in the Great Gesture and the Great Perfection points of view, and he taught predominantly the Six Dharmas of Naropa. He built temples everywhere for the accumulation of merit for all sentient beings, and he had many students. More than one hundred of them were waiting for us in his house. I entered his shrine room and saw a towering yogi with a long white beard—so magnificent. He held a bundle of smoking incense and a long white scarf to welcome me. We bowed and exchanged scarves, according to Dharma custom. When we use long white scarves, the length is symbolic of continuity. The white color is symbolic of pure intention; of faith when we offer them to statues, of devotion when we offer them to teachers, of respect when we offer them to parents, and of love when we offer them to friends. Then we sat and drank auspicious, welcoming tea and ate rice, talking in a formal style; but my mind was searching for that exotic girl.

My future mother-in-law was there. She also came from Dragonland. Her name was Glorious Prosperous Wish, and her charm was legendary. She had a well-proportioned body with clear, fair skin. The

Lopön Sönam Sangpo Rinpoche
(Exalted Instructor of Noble Destiny).

Triple Gems were her most precious, comforting companions, and she was always making offerings with rituals for the accumulation of merit. She had a very fortunate life; whatever she did was successful. She could do impossible things.

She had first been married to a wealthy landowner and had two sons with him, but she was really interested in following Dharma and not so interested in being a landowner's wife. She had faith, love, and devotion toward many lamas, especially to my father-in-law. Her older brother-in-law instigated her husband to be against her by constantly making him jealous. One day, after her husband asked her to come into his room, he locked the latch when she entered so that no one could prevent him from beating her. He beat her until her urine came. After he had stopped, she asked him to come to their shrine room with her. He innocently followed. She took an image case with a deity inside, and placing it on her head vowed loudly, "In this life I no longer wish to be your wife, but I pray that we will always support each other to benefit

25

our children and to serve the Dharma." Then she immediately escaped from the house, fearful that he might prevent her from leaving, and went to the upper temple called Golden Basin. She stayed there with some women friends until she was healed. Many times people asked her to rejoin with her former husband, and many times she answered, "I would like to be with a lama." Afterward, she brought a lovely young relative to her husband to take care of him in her place, and then joined my father-in-law, serving him with whatever he needed, helping to renovate old temples, build new temples, and make statues in many places for her whole life.

In Kathmandu, many years later, I dreamt of my mother-in-law after she had been cured from a long illness. A lovely white swan was in my hands. She transformed into a peacock, and turning her head away from me, she made a parasol of her feathers and seemed to say, "Goodbye." I said to a student who was near me, "She is going to die; bring milk quickly," but while he ran to bring milk, the bird's eyes and tongue became red, and she died. My heart felt crushed, and when I woke up it was still beating with sharp pains. After two days, I got a message from Dragonland that she had passed away.

———

At the time I was first in Dragonland, I spent every day with my future parents-in-law. At night I rested in a separate little house nearby where arrangements had been made for me. We became closer and closer. After about one month, my friend asked me, "Do you want to invite Smooth Melodious Lamp of Dharma to your residence?" And I said, "Yes." She came one night after dinner. She put a cup on my table and kneeled politely and shyly, filling it from a bottle of homemade liquor. We talked a little bit. When I said, "Now I want to sleep; do you want to sleep here?" she didn't answer, but with gracious smiling, she stayed.

It isn't necessary to think that silence is no answer. Sometimes silence is more profound than speaking and shows deeper love than flattering words. When All-Knowing Buddha's disciples asked him, "What is the absolute truth?" his answer was silence beyond substance words, vastly more profound than speaking.

An old lama with a thick mustache known as Yellow Lama, who

On horseback, 1980.

was my father-in-law's nephew by marriage, had been hoping for a long time to make a match between us. He thought he would be the one to introduce us. One day he came to me and said very seriously, "Now we must talk and decide how you two can meet. Soon it will be too late." When I said, "We have already been together for several weeks," he was shocked. "What?" he said, "Are you sure?" I said, "I'm positive." He turned his face and glared at me. Then he interrogated me like a criminal investigator with frowning eyes. "How? Who brought her here? Did she come alone or did you go to her?" After I explained clearly what had happened, he said, "Too fast, too fast," and he looked disappointed that he had not been the matchmaker.

On a day when the constellations were auspicious, we made a ceremony with rituals and offerings joined by many groups of people in front of a big altar in my father-in-law's temple. My wife gave me a silver platter inlaid with gold, decorated with mounds symbolic of the mandala of pure phenomena. She wound a long silk scarf around my neck and bowed with respect.

Later, she told me that in her childhood she had found a nine-pointed vajra when she was playing near her uncle's house. She showed it to her mother, who told her to keep it. I told her it was symbolic of meeting me, a follower of the nine yanas' precious teachings. Laughing, she told me not to make predictions through my conceit.

My wife has a very discreet and monogamous nature. She likes to make offerings and invite lamas, owing to the good habits of her parents. She isn't arrogant and doesn't like to flatter people. She is never unscrupulous in a worldly way for the benefit of her family, but only likes to support them in an honest and direct way. She has a noble, introspective, thorough style in whatever she does. Her mind is very clear and intuitive in automatically understanding the nature of other people's minds.

I never tire when we talk, because her voice is so soft, smooth, and gentle. When she speaks peacefully, her manner is naturally comforting, with pure and deep meaning that touches the heart, but sometimes when she gets angry at me because of my reverse activities, she scares me more than a fascist.

We spent a few years in the Hidden Fern Valley, Padmasambhava's blessed place, where we had met. In the beautiful, dense forests and rocky mountains, it was always drizzling, and near a cool, green-colored river whose banks were covered with pearly pebbles and gold powdered sand, there were three different natural hot springs. The middle hot spring was three hours from our main residence. Its name was Occurrence of All Benefits and Qualities. Once I went on retreat with my wife, her aunt, and two cats nearby in the forest, on an enormous rocky mountain called Auspicious Sky-Touching Castle. I practiced in a log cabin that was built for me there. My wife and her aunt prepared offerings for the altar and meals for me between periods of practice.

With bow and arrow.

Once her aunt was stung on the nose by a bee, and I kept laughing at her swelling nose until my wife got angry with me for being disrespectful.

After a while, a hermit arrived to receive teachings from me. There was a big tree near our house, which he hollowed out at the base to build a retreat room for himself to do dakini practice. He made a ceiling, walls, and floor inside the tree. It was amazingly beautiful. One day the top of the tree cracked off and fell down with a loud crash because it was too heavy for the hollowed-out trunk to support. When we heard the noise and anxiously came rushing out, the hermit stepped out of his house unharmed and jokingly boasted, "The ego tree was disturbing me, so I visualized cutting it off with my wisdom curved knife."

Usually, when the retreats were finished, we would stay there for a few days. Then my wife and I would climb down alone in the evening to the shore of the river and take natural hot-spring baths. Sometimes things appear more mysteriously beautiful at night than in the day. When the moon rose, we would look at each other's body in the pool and talk about the body's proportions. Then, holding hands, we would silently listen to the river's soothing sound.

As it says in the *Anguta Sutra,*

> There is infinite beauty in the universe, but the most beautiful sight to the eyes of a man is the form of a woman, and to the eyes of a woman, the most beautiful sight is the form of a man. There is no beauty superior to this.
>
> The most harmonious sound to the ears of a man is the voice of a woman, and to the ears of a woman, the most harmonious sound is the voice of a man. There is no sound superior to this.
>
> The most exquisite smell to the nose of a man is the scent of a woman, and to the nose of a woman, the most exquisite smell is the scent of a man. There is no smell superior to this.
>
> The most delicious flavor to the mouth of a man is the taste of a woman, and to the mouth of a woman, the most delicious flavor is the taste of a man. There is no flavor superior to this.
>
> The most pleasing sensation to the body of a man is the touch of a woman, and to the body of a woman, the most pleasing sensation is the touch of a man. There is no sensation superior to this.
>
> The most desirable feeling to the heart of a man is the love of a woman, and to the heart of a woman, the most desirable feeling is the love of a man. There is no feeling superior to this.

When we returned, we would have dinner with aged rice wine, which the people from the region say is very nourishing after a hot bath. Sometimes we would climb up in the daytime and raise prayer flags, filling the sky with incense offerings of smoking juniper to link with deities.

Later, we had three sweetheart daughters and four sweetheart sons. We are both praying that these children will be joined to the Dharma, which is always meaningful, and will serve all sentient beings with vast intention.

When there was war between Supreme Shakya Sphere and Wisdom Sword Holder's Land, to be safe, my wife and I left Dragonland with my parents-in-law to go to Supreme Shakya Sphere. The Noble Lama Indestructible Great Bliss helped us find work to support ourselves at an air message generator, speaking in the languages of Snowland and Dragonland. This was north of the blessed stupa that marks the enlightenment of the Buddha Shakyamuni.

Indestructible Great Bliss was eccentric in a saintly way. Often people were paranoid about his unusual words and activity, which were abnormal to normal, ordinary people. For instance, one time my sister was about to have a year of obstacles according to the Snowland calendar. When she asked him if there would be any problems in her life, he wrote a prophecy that said, "Your obstacles of the next year will be purified by fucking." She was so angry and upset, throwing his letter into my hand and asking me, "What is this crazy lama saying with these rude words?" I said, "This will be true, because his predictions are reliable. Anyway, we cannot judge what he says, so maybe it is too early to get upset without knowing what will happen next year." The next year, she unexpectedly met her new husband and they joined and had a baby, and she had no obstacles. When I reminded her of what this lama had predicted, she accepted his accuracy with astonishment.

Also, one Westerner asked him, "What is the easiest and fastest way to attain enlightenment?" He answered, "If you fuck one hundred dakinis, I guarantee that you will never be reborn in lower realms."

At that time, I read the history of Mahatma Gandhi and saw pictures of his skeletal body, like Milarepa's ascetic form. It seemed as if the high, cool Snow Mountain Land saint had come out of his cave again to go to the low, hot plains to make peace for the world's sorrowful beings in the unlucky degenerate age.

Whenever I saw his picture, my heart would fill with praise for his precious noble qualities and I would think: many world leaders have outwardly straight bodies and inwardly crooked minds. Outwardly,

31

your body is bent, but inwardly your mind is straight. They keep their clothes clean, but they cannot clean their minds. They cover their bodies with elaborate formal costumes; your iron-colored body is wrapped only in a piece of simple white cloth. They go fearfully with many bodyguards from place to place in their private cars and planes; you go fearlessly from place to place sharing the transportation of ordinary people. They kill hundreds of animals for entertainment, devouring the red meat that provides only one meal's flavor; you keep one living goat, which provides white milk for all of your meals. Outwardly, they talk about peace for their country while inwardly trying to make war for their profit. Outwardly, you try to make peace for all nations while inwardly trying to bring harmony to your own country. In order to destroy foreign countries, they make bombs that they cannot use without destroying themselves, and their dangerous war-weapons accumulate for generations, increasing fear. Your continuous, kind love-weapon penetrates throughout the world, creating peace and understanding. When they die, their precious possessions stay behind in a Swiss bank, causing family feuds. When you died you left behind just one old walking stick and went freely in the ten directions of the Bodhisattvas' land, leaving the gift of your Bodhisattva actions. Please come back again and again to douse the flames of violent beings with the nectar of your kind and peaceful speech and actions.

Later, when I went back to East Dragonland with my wife and children, we couldn't go to Upper Valley of Amusement, so we just stayed in Above Auspicious Land. Dragonland is a very small country between Supreme Shakya Sphere and Snowland. It has many different climates. Close to the border of Snowland, there are forests and rocky mountains. It is high, the people's complexions are healthy, and the skies are open. Many nomads live in the high places with wild deer and tamed yaks. Close to the border of Supreme Shakya Sphere, there are jungles with wild elephants and tigers, pythons and poisonous snakes, wolves, and tame cows. Higher up, the grass is mostly green-gray and the gray mountains are covered with many pines. There are rivers, waterfalls, and blessed holy caves, including one called Tiger's Lair. Near Tiger's Lair is a waterfall that has rainbows in its mist. There are also many monasteries and temples filled with images, and toward the direction of the sunrise there is a holy cave called Lion's Castle where Padmasambhava manifested the mandala of glorious Vajra Kumara.

With Bhutanese dancers.

For many years, Padmasambhava, Victorious Great Powerful Empowerment of Speech, and many other saints and wise persons blessed Dragonland. The religious traditions there are predominantly the Old School lineage of the Great Perfection and the New School lineage of the Great Gesture. Even though this is the unlucky degenerate age, parents in Dragonland still try to teach their children from earliest childhood to go to temples, receive blessings, have respect for holy beings, make offerings, and recite the mantras of Padmasambhava and Avalokiteshvara.

I had started to read some Dharma to others when I was nineteen years old and had begun further teaching from the age of twenty-four. I traveled many times in Supreme Shakya Sphere and had different spiritual friends in different places. I especially traveled in the North and East, and later, when I became sick, I had to spend time in several medicine houses there.

There are many holy places blessed by Lord Buddha's feet in Supreme Shakya Sphere. The country is divided into several states that have many different cultures and wonderful customs that exclude modern style. In general, the way of the women there is beautiful, recalling the feminine wisdom deities in their ancient art.

Gazing beyond a valley of rice fields in Nepal.

My sickness didn't heal, so friends of friends invited me to the West for treatment. When I left, my mother-in-law said good-bye. "Please don't get attached to developed countries' modern phenomena. Come back soon to our simple, natural country to help the Dharma." My wife was sad and wept in front of me in the backyard of our winter house. When we said good-bye, she prayed and said to me, "I hope in my life I never hear that Thinley Norbu has passed away." (Instead, it was I who heard that she had passed away. After traveling to our elder daughter's house in Switzerland to receive medical treatment, she later passed away from diabetes in Bhutan.)

Then I left to say good-bye to my mother, who lived in Supreme Shakya Sphere. "Definitely," she said, "you are not going to die. I will pray to Tara and she will protect you. You will become healthy again and we will see each other soon." Later, as she said, we met many times.

I traveled to Buddha's Toe-Petal Blossom Land to say good-bye to my father. I had been there a few times before. The first time, many years ago, my mother, brother, half sister, and I had gone there on a pilgrimage. We went in a manmade sky bird, and after we were already in the air, my mother asked me to tell the pilot to return immediately. She had a headache and vomiting sensation. In general, she hated to go by manmade sky bird or in anything that moved by a motor. We explained to her that we couldn't tell the pilot to return, that it was a government sky bird, that there were many other passengers and rules, that he couldn't stop for just one person, and that the sky bird didn't belong to us. She was angry. She jabbed me with her elbow and said in a loud voice, "Eat shit!"

Many of the people of Buddha's Toe-Petal Blossom Land are followers of the Hindu religion. At certain times they will kill countless animals as offerings to Mahadeva, and on those days blood is scattered everywhere, especially on Mahadeva's image. Also, many of the people are followers of Buddhism, and at certain times, flowers are scattered everywhere as offerings to all Buddhas' and Bodhisattvas' images.

After spending some time with my father, I finally left for the West. Some friends had invited me to Emerald Buddha Land, and I spent a few weeks there discussing practice in a simple way. They took me by

In Thailand (Emerald Buddha Land), with offerings of flowers, 1986.

boat to some sacred places with many lakes full of pink lotuses and white ducks. We went to see the famous Emerald Buddha, offered flowers, prostrated, prayed, and meditated together. Many Buddhists were praying and meditating, while many unreligious tourists sat on the floor with curiosity.

One time, a blue-eyed, blond-eyebrowed friend took us to a bar where two young women brought us grain spirits to drink. Before drinking, I made an offering prayer. One of these young women, noticing my gesture, showed me a Buddhist medallion she was wearing, so we offered together and then drank together. She was very natural and lovely. Even though we were both Easterners, we couldn't speak the same language, so I praised her silently.

Beauty face,
complexion glowing like the full moon,
eyes of a young deer
awakened by the rustle of a gentle wind,
your brows outstretched,
night blue seagull wings
sailing the open sky.
When you linger, your fine
thick lashes rest
like a young fawn suckling milk.

Sparkling teeth in lined perfection,
white pearls shining,
red lotus lips smile
with fresh-smelling sweet nectar.
Black silken hair flows loosely
over your straight shoulders
and smooth, flat back.

Fine neck slender as a white swan
swaying from side to side,
your sounds soothing the saddened heart
like the flute of Gandharva's daughter,
words comforting the sorrowed mind
like a poem with the message of Saraswati.

Smooth, round breasts,
rising form like conch shells
full with love.
Firm young willow trunk,
thighs conquering all
who gaze toward your hidden glen,
your buttocks like sweet mounds
curving into endless space.

Secret flowering desire's smiling dew,
merely to touch your honey pollen
melts them to the mysterious island
of all the Buddhas.

From Emerald Buddha Land, I flew to France, where my friends picked me up at the airfield and took me to their house in Paris. Paris is an elegant paradise city appearing on this earth like a beautiful fantasy mandala with ornamented buildings, outdoor sculpture, and many cars running on the open cobblestoned streets, which seem joined to the sky.

The French are inscrutable in a different way than the Orientals. They are always concerned with good manners, and almost everybody's clothes are very clean. They have many different types of ripened grape spirits competing for long life in dark cellars, and countless cheeses, considered the most delicious in the world, keeping many years' retreat and holding their rot vows until their skin grows gray fur. They try to make the most rotten-smelling cheese and the most

In Paris, at the Arc de Triomphe, 1982.

Teaching Dharma in New York City, 1979.

fresh-smelling perfume. Of course, in samsara, we are always jumping
between confusing contradictions, and so we distract ourselves with
rotten and sweet.

My friends took care of me like a precious brother. They showed
me many libraries and museums with rare antique religious objects.
These ancient religious objects once were natural, wonderful, and
alive, but sometimes I felt sad to look at them because now they each
seemed to be just a name and a decoration. In the West, there are large
libraries and museums everywhere, but the quality of the energy in
these buildings is different than in the East, where the precious objects
inside buildings are worshiped. I thought, people may gather priceless
objects from all over the world, but if they are concerned only with
substance, the objects will become inert. Without the presence of deity's essence, the deity's splendid energy is absent.

In Nepal, Rinpoche paints a statue of Guru Rinpoche (Padmasambhava) that he designed.

In the East, from ancient times, magic smiths and wisdom masters blessed by deities have performed consecration ceremonies invoking deities to empower their images. Empowered images have spiritual wisdom essence, and their owners continuously show their deep respect by making prayers and offerings to them. When favorable circumstances come together, and the karmic connection is made between faith and the wisdom deity's blessing, these images automatically become alive and splendid through the energy of pure phenomena and pure faith.

When the deity is invoked, there is a prayer: "Whenever there is violence coming from the elements or from beings, please depart from these statues or paintings to your pureland." Even though Western countries keep many priceless antiques in museums, they have lost their lively and splendid quality because of substance thinking, and they are valued only as material objects such as fancy paperweights, or cigarette and candle holders; there is no idea of having respect for their spiritual essence and no question of making prayers and offerings to them. So, the antique images are imprisoned with high insurance in museum showcases, and their lively energy, which had been invoked in ancient times, has departed.

On the streets in Paris or on the sidewalks in front of the elegant shops and cafés, many stylish young handsome men proudly walk, and butter-skinned, clear-eyed women with blond or dark hair glamorously flirt and tantalize. In some parks in the city, many old gentlemen with thick coats, sticks, and hats and many old gentleladies are walking straight with their heads up, rarely turning down or to the side.

My French friends are very kind and especially devoted to Buddhism and Padmasambhava's teachings. During my first trip to France, we didn't speak the same language, so we often communicated with gestures. Sometimes I think it is better not to know a language. Rather than talking, it is better to reserve energy through silence. But most Westerners try to look intelligent through talking and think silence is uncomfortable, so it is better to be talkative if you want to spend time in the West. Of course, since human beings have dualistic tongue, everything that is said is an impetuous expression of incurable, contagious blurting. We who have ordinary limited qualities incessantly chatter, while those with limitless wisdom qualities remain silent. It is like the difference between the movement of shallow water and the stillness of the deepest sea. Western people have many fine qualities, like the rapid waters of mountain rivers, but they cannot put out the blazing fire of their mouth.

In Europe, I traveled to Amsterdam, but I couldn't spend a long time there. It is a sensual, sweet canal city—so beautiful. People are free and fresh, friendly and warm even to strangers.

I also traveled to Switzerland, a beautiful country that they say is neutral and beyond extremes. Of course, this is the best if it is beneficial and not dull. I went to doctors in Lausanne and Geneva. Everything was very clean, but if I had stayed longer, I might not have been able to adapt to cuckoo's time with my senile mind.

I had been invited to the United States, and on my way I stopped for a few weeks in London, which is a very grand, dignified city. A lady journalist, a very kind, intelligent, serious practitioner who had recently become a nun, invited me to stay at her house. I lived on the first floor in the room with the altar with many strong-smelling small dogs.

Sometimes I walked in Hyde Park near her house. On certain vacation days, people gather there and demand what they need by giving lectures. Some people insult the Queen, some praise the royal family, some insult communists, some praise capitalists, some insult religion, some praise Dharma. Young girls and good-looking, cleanly dressed

In London, 1980.

people in riding costumes can be seen on their horses galloping in the park between weeping willows, the horses beating their hooves on the ground like African drums.

On the avenue, especially near the Queen's palace, there are tall police with black hats and long guns. They stand in small guardhouses that look like copies of standing coffins made to fit their bodies exactly. They never move. If you do not watch carefully, you can misunderstand and think they are mannequins of soldiers. When I peeped through the gate of the palace, I did not notice they were living beings until they hit the rings on their thumbs against their guns as a signal to tell me to stop peeping.

On the streets of New York City, 1982.

My journey's style was very smooth through the grace of Padma-sambhava. Even though I couldn't speak foreign languages, wherever I went, my friends helped me to go easily from place to place and from land to land.

I flew from the city of London in the Western continent to the city of New York in the Far Western continent. An American spiritual friend came to the airfield to fetch me. We had heard each other's names before but we had never seen each other, so when he saw me after I had finished going through customs, he folded his hands around his long, white scarf in Snowland welcoming style, giving me a sign to recognize him from the other side of the customs check booth. Then we introduced ourselves.

In Hawaii, 1977, wearing glasses made with crystal lenses
given to Rinpoche by Kyabje Dudjom Rinpoche.

He had spent a long time in India studying Tibetan Buddhism with his teachers there. His noble high-standard style was very gentle and precise. He took me to a hotel and showed me to the room that he had arranged for me to stay in, and the next day we flew by airplane to his house in Massachusetts, where we spent some time.

After a while, I visited Lotus Island on the West Coast, where the master with an Asian body and a Western teacher's mind lives. I spent some time there and then left for Honolulu in the Hawaiian Islands. It has a very modern city landscape, not crowded like most cities, but very open, spacious, and clean. The hills are low-lying and gently sloping, with many small white houses resting in their valley laps. Many bright-colored flowering trees were planted everywhere, particularly the golden shower tree. In the endless turquoise ocean waves, many young men and women were swimming and surfing. In the endless blue sky, many hang gliders were soaring.

One day a friend took me to a house in the country outside of Honolulu. This house sat on top of a smooth hill that swelled fully like a young woman's breast. The walls were transparent glass, and wherever I looked, the ocean stretched endlessly, seeming to flow onto me. As much as I looked toward the ocean to find its end, that much the ocean's phenomena seemed to extend endlessly farther and farther until it joined with the endless sky. There was no more mountain, no more earth, no more division between ocean, sky, mind; ocean, sky, and mind became one color. Through this vast outer object expanse, momentarily my boundless inner subject mind disappeared into one edgeless space of turquoise light. Where I was, where the ocean was, where the sky was, I couldn't understand, but still it was clear, but still it was profound, but still it was open.

Then I remembered Samantabhadra and prayed:

O Samantabhadra
in the world
everyone knows sea
everyone knows sky.
No one knows you
no one knows me.

O Samantabhadra
may I know you
may you know me.

O Samantabhadra
may I thank you
though you are unthankable.
May I believe in you
though you are unbelievable.

Samantabhadra, in a painting by Phende Norbu Rinpoche.

There are many regions in the United States, and in each one the people have different habits and styles, but in general the habits of their minds are very similar. This is true because through its karma, the country is vast and rich with many natural resources; through its many great inventors, its wealth and technology have grown and progressed; and through democratic government, the people have been able to express their hopes freely. These three causes have led to technological machine living, resulting in a rich and easy lifestyle. For this reason, according to worldly phenomena, Americans became the most materially powerful in the world in this generation. Because they have unobstructed possibilities for creating countless substance things, everyone's mind can become a substance creator. They are so diligently and persistently making substance creations with speedy competition mind that they put their energy totally into creating visible and tangible external substance. This emphasis is the cause of the American what's-happening-figure-out mind.

I thought, in some ways, according to the worldly view, they seemingly have an easy, comfortable life. Transportation under the cities in the subway is easy; transportation on land in buses is easy; transportation through the sky in airplanes is easy. If you want to have a cold meal, it is easy to take it out of the refrigerator instantly. If you want to have a hot meal, it is easy to cook it on the stove or in the microwave oven instantly. If you want to shop, it is easy to put your groceries in a shopping cart and to buy from the computer cashier instantly. If you are cold in the wintertime, it is easy to be warm in your house with central heating. If you are hot in the summertime, it is easy to be cool in your house with air-conditioning instantly. If you want to talk to someone, it is easy to call them on the telephone instantly. If you are lonely and want company, it is easy to turn on the television and choose the channel you desire to be entertained by commercials instantly. As they say, "Take it easy."

But in order to make substance qualities dependable, machine mind automatically isolates the outer elements from the inner elements and, separated from their inner elements' energy, the outer elements become impoverished and dried. The lifeless, hard cement on the street hurts lively, sensitive feet. The lifeless, dry heat in the house ages lively, sensitive skin. The lifeless gas lines of the stove dull lively, sensitive taste. The lifeless electric refrigerator cold fades lively, sensitive flavor. The lifeless, speedy television stories deaden the lively, sensitive mind.

Of course, if mechanical energy were inexhaustible, the substance qualities of mechanical inventions could help inexhaustibly. But ultimately, machines have only inert, external substance power, and since by nature substance changes, and by nature outer energy diminishes, "take it easy" sometimes becomes the cause of being hard to take. As they say, "I can't take it."

Through constant reliance on machines, a person develops the habit of separating inner, invisible, intangible elements from outer, visible, tangible elements. As a result of this separation habit, no energy is gathered within, and all substance is eventually exhausted without. When outer substance qualities are exhausted, the mind, spoiled by reliance on the instant comfort of mechanical inventions, also becomes exhausted. In this way, the temporary, inert encouragement of machines is eventually the cause of discouragement.

So, when a machine's energy is exhausted, causing a mechanical breakdown, the mind that depends on it also becomes exhausted, causing a nervous breakdown, because unlike unending, dependable natural mind, a machine gives only temporary benefits, and cannot be relied on to comfort deeply and long-lastingly with inexhaustible natural qualities.

Then, when the temporary benefits are exhausted, depression comes and people say, "Why do anything? Nothing makes sense." But this is depression. It is not like the practitioner's view of the weariness of samsara. The sadness is that this idea that nothing makes sense is just left there. They do not know how to go from "nothing makes sense" to making sense, due to not believing in a spiritual way.

Because America is a relatively new country, it doesn't have a long history. Because Americans don't have a long history, they don't respect lineage and are actually proud of not depending on a lineage. But it is not possible to learn anything without depending on a lineage.

In America, because children do not learn respect for lineage, they feel free to insult and dishonor their parents and teachers. They have the freedom to publicly criticize and even slander the people who taught them and who were kind to them. Even if parents made mistakes, children should still respect them, since they gave them a precious human birth. Even if teachers made mistakes, students should still respect them, since they taught them the point of view of what is wrong and right in order to increase their intelligence. If they respect parents and teachers, then when they become parents and teachers, they can benefit children or students in future generations by keeping the lineage of noble qualities.

In America, there are many students and teachers from the Buddhist tradition who also don't understand or respect lineage. Actually, all teaching comes from unbroken lineage and all wisdom qualities come from teaching, from the student honoring and respecting the teacher through love and devotion.

Telephoning from Berkeley, 1977.

If students study Buddhism, which comes from another country, they must respect the spiritual traditions of that country in order to have pure lineage in a vast way. If students don't want to depend on other countries' religious ideas, this is stupid since almost all Americans originally came from other nations. If they want to ignore lineage or disconnect from it, this is like a praying mantis who bites off her mate's head after sex.

In America, there are also many praying mantis spiritual teachers who prefer to nationalize their religious ideas according to American fashion rather than respecting their religion's original lineage. Instead of changing lineage, they can adapt and adjust to their situation, but the main idea is that you cannot change lineage. For example, if an American learns karate from Japan, then the body of the karate fighter has changed, not the lineage of karate. They should respect the teacher without being racist, but the praying mantis way of teaching is actually racist; it cannot give sublime blessings with pure lineage prayers.

In California, 1976, with Kyabje Dudjom Rinpoche,
who asked Rinpoche to go to the West to teach.

Buddha's pure wisdom lineage holders are nonracist. This is compatible with the meaning of the Dharma teaching to benefit all beings equally. Pure Buddhist tradition doesn't exclude anyone, whether they have blond hair and blue eyes or brown hair and brown eyes. Rather than having a physical lineage, they must have wisdom spiritual lineage.

Because this country is very new to Dharma, and because these new American students have freedom habits, they often betray their teacher. Instead of respecting their teacher, they are excited to take revenge as they go from Dharma center to Dharma center and from teacher to teacher. This is not the proper way. Even farmers want their cows and horses to have good lineage, but these practitioners of this degenerate age think they don't need a pure lineage. Many students in America are only learning Dharma for their credentials and status rather than having real faith and devotion to hold a pure lineage with the positive intention of attaining enlightenment in order to benefit all sentient beings.

With Kyabje Dilgo Khyente Rinpoche (All-Knowing Loving Auspicious Majestic Accomplishment) in Parping, Nepal.

With Kyabje Chadral Rinpoche in Rinpoche's residence in Nepal, 1995.

With Kyabje Dodrup Rinpoche in Kunzang Gatshal,
Rinpoche's retreat land in upstate New York, 1994.

With Kyabje Penor Rinpoche in Kunzang Gatshal, 2000.

*Reading fortune cookie messages with Kyabje Dudjom Rinpoche
in New York, 1978. (Photo © Les Levine.)*

According to Dharma tradition, if someone is a teacher, he is not ordinary, but connected to Buddha, which causes enlightenment. When one takes refuge, one takes the vow that until attaining enlightenment, one will never abandon the Triple Gems, and one's teacher is the representative of the Triple Gems. But from their freedom idea, people from the Land of Opportunity can turn against teachers. While their teacher is living, they seem to respect him and listen to teachings from him, but when their teacher passes, they think they can write anything about him, since through their nihilist habit, they think their teacher is finished. They can make false accusations and print books for sale identifying their teacher and saying disgusting words about his personal qualities, which is totally against Dharma tradition. They did not understand Dharma, and that their teacher is the representative of the Buddhas, and that Buddhas never die. They did not believe.

Holding drum and bell, in Bhutan, 1976.

Who can be a teacher and who cannot be a teacher is only known from wisdom scholars, those who are highly realized, and the omniscient Buddhas. It is a personal connection that does not come from a decision made at the meeting of a group, because it is not a social idea. Social ideas exist at a worldly level and will change. Some people want to create what they call an American Buddhism, but these American Buddhists have learned from Tibetans, and Tibetans learned from Indians. Trying not to depend on another country's lineage, even though it is the lineage of origin, becomes racist. By being prejudiced, they call some teachers Eastern teachers and some teachers Western teachers. But basically, the actual, pure idea of Dharma is not being racist. They think if they learn something from somewhere, they can mix it with their own country's tradition, making something up. People who do not respect actual true lineage can do anything. If they believe in pure Dharma, they must have lineage. If they say that they can create their own Dharma, how are they going to go back to their lineage? For example, Dharma from an Indian lineage flourished among Tibetan people, who respected Indian Buddhist lineage holders such as Tilopa and Naropa. Without respecting Indians, what would their lineage of initiations and meditation be?

Somehow, through my karmic connection to America, I am very concerned about Americans, especially my few special American friends, so I am wishing to wake them up.

———

America is often called the Land of Opportunity because the American Constitution grants so much freedom to its citizens. Even though in some ways this freedom is valuable, sometimes it becomes excessive and causes tremendous problems and chaos.

For example, the freedom to bear arms in America gives anyone the right to buy weapons in order to shoot Americans. Many gangsters come to the Land of Opportunity since they can buy guns freely and commit crimes freely. Many terrorists come to the Land of Opportunity since they can buy guns freely to create terror. So, everyone can shoot everyone else, which is no different from a small-scale war. America is considered to be a civilized country, but its Constitution protects people's right to keep guns. Americans have an extra unusual reputation in the world for continuous killing, from the killing of animals during hunting season, to murder within families, to racist phenomena, from individual killing to public genocide. This makes other countries think America is an uncivilized, savage country.

A few years ago, when a hunter killed a woman who had stepped out of her door into her own yard, the judge and jury found the hunter innocent because the woman was not wearing red to warn the hunter not to shoot her in her own yard. It is unbelievable, but it looks as if in the Land of Opportunity, according to the American Constitution, a homeowner cannot step from her own door into her own yard during the hunting season without risking her life. The criminal becomes innocent and the innocent become criminal.

In some communist countries, they used to prohibit the sale of guns, so at least there was less robbery and murder. In America, the right to bear arms and the freedom to buy guns actually backfire, like a man getting his mustache burned when he blows out the candles on his birthday cake.

The police cannot even protect the public, so the public's right to have guns causes continuous criminal activity. Through the idea of freedom, Americans can invite anti-American enemy terrorists to their own

*On porch in Wyoming, 1978, during several
weeks of teachings given there.*

country and train them how to shoot back at their own heads. Through idiotic political leaders, the government can support its enemies, and through greedy company leaders, it can make many weapons to sell to its own enemies. In general, according to a worldly manner, one good human quality in the history of ancient countries is loyalty. But Americans, from individuals up to the government, have betrayal habit from lack of discipline and excessive freedom. They are not ashamed to betray anyone if it benefits them because of their habit of expedience. Even though America is a large country with material wealth, because Americans do not have the qualities of nobility and dignity, America becomes like a business station. Because of this, other countries' reaction is to treat America cheaply even when America supports them. I am saying this with good intention, worrying for Americans. Government officials are ready to leak secrets to the media to betray their own government for their own purposes, and the media are ready to publicize their own government's faults to the nation and to the world, to make others excited so they will listen to them, in order to make a reputation and money for themselves. The media sometimes call this public service, but they are rarely thinking of how to benefit, visualizing themselves as television actors and actresses as they report the news.

Even though the media have the potential to benefit, those working in the media often create issues, interference, and disturbance between the government and people, and between family and friends, for the benefit of their jobs and for profit. For example, there is often talk about gun control in the media, but so much violence is shown on television that children are influenced to become violent later and buy guns. Even though parents have good intentions to educate their children with all the best positive phenomena, their children are still influenced by the negative phenomena on television.

There are so many important international issues that should be broadcast in the news to educate young people in order to make better communication in the world, but instead, the media are always reporting about murder and rape. Because other countries have certain traditions of their own, it is difficult to be compatible with America's lack of versatility and spoiled, commanding ego, which comes from their own country's habit of freedom. If, instead, the media brought knowledge of many different cultures to America, teaching people to communicate with others, they would develop America's culture in an appropriate way and make Americans less parochial, more versatile, and harmonious in the world. Then Americans would not only think of the American view, imposing it on other nations, and internationally there would not be the frequent problems that there are now.

In this Land of Opportunity, there is so much freedom that citizens can even burn their own nation's flag that symbolizes their nation's dignity and unity. If these flag-burners don't want to respect their nation's honor and want excessive freedom, they should go to live with beasts, where there are no flags.

The misinterpretation of individual freedom and independence is a big problem in America. Americans are often proud of their freedom from surrender and dependency, thinking they are better than any other civilized country.

Because, from childhood, Americans are not strictly disciplined or taught respect by their parents and teachers, their adult behavior is often chaotic, disrespectful, and harmful. For example, when they travel to other countries, rather than adapting to and obeying the laws there, they use only their own ego's lawless laws. Some years ago, an American boy was caned in Singapore as a punishment for making graffiti there. One small country beat one biggest country's boy because of that boy's misunderstanding and abuse of freedom. The only way he could be released from Singapore was through surrendering to the punishment.

Even though Japan bombed China and America equally during the war, later Japan apologized to China but refused to apologize to America since Japan thought of America as a newborn baby who doesn't need an apology.

In the West, women have wanted more and more freedom and so have engaged in the feminist movement, saying that men and women should be equal. Of course, in order to better their country and help other beings without seeding hatred between men and women, it is right for women to have equal education, equal pay, and equal job opportunities, including being equally able to run for president. According to the Mahayana system, all sentient beings have the same Buddha nature, so since women and men are the same human beings, why can't women have the same opportunities as men to use all of their mind's qualities freely?

Even so, in some ways women and men do not have the same opportunities because from the beginning their energies are different from each other as a result of their previous karma. For example, according to outer phenomena, in the worldly system men are usually physically stronger, so they can do certain kinds of heavy work more easily than women. Yet according to inner phenomena in the inner tantric system, women have more magic mind power with sensitivity than men, so they are closer to the source of phenomena.

If women could be wise and plan to ultimately benefit all beings, they would also naturally liberate themselves, like Sublime Tara. But sometimes, just like men, women try to excessively increase their temporary ordinary power and make many banal issues into big issues, making vinegar energy without thinking how to increase their positive

At Swayambhu Stupa, with women disciples from Ladakh, 1986.

honey energy and pure wisdom power. Women lose their attractive feminine aspect and become weird, even walking like marching Nazi soldiers, scaring all men. As a result, both men and women may use each other only temporarily for pleasure since they have no interest in the continuous power of spiritual energy's extraordinary love. So, love between men and women may turn into a power struggle.

In this life, because of karmic result, some beings took a female body. If they don't like their body, they can pray that in their next life they will be reborn with a man's body rather than doing bodybuilding exercises in order to create and exhibit a powerful male body with veins and bulging muscles. Many of these bodybuilder women start to organize palm-rubbing phenomena with each other, or buy lifeless dildos, the color of uncooked chicken. Instead of this, if they can create a graceful, beautiful, refined female body, they will be able to be naturally alluring to men, which will give them natural power instead of equality. Many American gentlemen are afraid of these powerful bodybuilding ladies, so they run away to other men to dig shit, just as many years ago people came from everywhere to the Land of Opportunity to dig gold, thinking this is their unassailable right.

Just because men and women are born with different bodies doesn't mean that one is superior or inferior to the other. They are just different, so instead of trying to compare or compete with each other physically, pushing to be equal or better, which often creates negative energy, women should learn to cooperate with men in order to create balance and harmony and positive energy within family and country. Even if women want to have physical equality with men, how could female athletes compete with male athletes instead of with each other? How could one strong heavyweight female boxer fight with someone like Mike Tyson for the championship?

Because of this equality idea, the American government has considered the right of women to engage in military combat. But this is a wrong right rather than a right right. It is unnecessary for women to risk their lives in a war in combat that relies on physical strength, which is different between men and women, when there are so many other opportunities for them to serve their country and benefit others graciously instead of aggressively. They can raise and educate children, and they can have many different kinds of meaningful professions, including political positions.

In feminism, the best role models women can have are Tara and Yeshe Tsogyal. But if they cannot be like them, they should try to be like Mother Teresa. And if they cannot be like her, they should at least try to be like Margaret Thatcher and Golda Meir, who were dignified political leaders who wisely protected their own countries and wisely communicated with other countries rather than quarreling about petty issues.

Sometimes feminist ideas cause hatred and anger toward men. For example, the news reported that many women congratulated a lady who killed a rapist. But these are reverse congratulations since they are influencing and encouraging other innocent women to commit murder and be criminals, making them lawless, which decreases the natural honor of women.

It is strange that Americans are so concerned about human rights in other countries, while in their own country they become lawless and uncivilized because of their excessive freedom, which often creates human wrongs instead of human rights. Through their anger, women feel they have the freedom to do anything. Because of the influence of women's rights, one lady cut off her husband's penis, just like cutting a sausage for dinner. Then she threw it into a field. It is ridiculous that even though policemen often cannot find criminals, they easily found the missing piece of his penis to bring back to the husband. It is wonderful that because of America's advanced medical technology, the penis was put back on the man. But I am worried that it is not working normally with a woman and that it might be dismantled again.

Some women are so angry at men that they don't want to depend on men for anything. If they decide to have children, they are proud that they don't need men and can just go to a sperm bank. But this sperm is from men and not from donkeys, so they still depend on men. Also, even if these women hate men, sometimes the sperm bank babies they have are boys who will become men.

Some American psychologists say that women hate men because they had bad fathers. Then, even though men are not like their fathers, they still hate them. Many psychologists have unwise and incorrect explanations about our behavior that only cause more hatred between human beings, which can seed problems for a whole country. But, of course, there are also good psychologists who benefit others. Many of them have nervous breakdowns and afterward treat patients who have nervous breakdowns.

Although men and women may think they will be free and have some power if they separate from each other, they usually suffer from loneliness as a result of their power struggles. Ordinary power must have an object in order to exist, so ordinary people lose their sense of power when they are alone. Rather than remain alone, they again seek out the comforting company of a new object. Of course, if they become good practitioners, they can learn to create real, unlosable spiritual power, and though they appear to be outwardly alone, inwardly they can be comforted by the companionship of their wisdom deity's appearance. Still, I am grateful that through this increased freedom idea, many women are more open to vast Dharma than before. But sometimes I am frightened by some terrifyingly arrogant and shallow women, and then I am reminded of the general Hinayana theory that to be born a woman is a lower birth. In any case, since I try to have faith in the inner Vajrayana view, which admires women as the support for increasing wisdom energy, I like to respect women and pray always, until I reach the state of Vajradhara, that I will be a wisdom hero who always has wisdom heroines with complementary energy as companions to attain desireless wisdom bliss.

At Namobuddha Stupa in Nepal, 1984.

Outwardly, Westerners may seem to have a good life, but inwardly they still suffer and have pain because they haven't learned how to use their minds.

In Buddhist countries, it is wonderful to often see old people believing in Buddha and interested in meditating, praying, resting, and watching their own natural, clear mirror mind through the blessing of

At the Gamri River in Rangjung, East Bhutan, 1995.

their guardian wisdom teacher in order to temporarily have less fear, frustration, and loneliness. Even those who are not practicing still have faith traditionally, so they at least have the aim to be born in higher realms or purelands, and to have some confidence at their final departure.

In non-Buddhist countries' modern tradition, it is sad to see old people sitting and reminiscing meaninglessly about whatever they used to be that is already gone and cannot be brought back, which causes more depression, unhappiness, frustration, and attachment. Although these memories cannot be brought back to life, at the same time they cannot be abandoned, and so these old people exhaust their own energy, becoming aimless at their final departure.

In America there are many different kinds of social classes, nation-

Smiling in Jorpati, Nepal.

alities, and cultural facades, but in general, through its free democratic tradition, parents and teachers teach children to speak freely, move freely, and act freely with direct and confident honesty.

In many Eastern countries there are strong traditions and people are often bound by fixed religious and worldly social customs. Through misunderstanding and misinterpretation, some Dharma customs are bound by many generations' habits, and so in some ways, even if they have the capacity, people cannot act freely, they cannot speak freely, and they cannot be free.

If they have patient minds, Westerners are in some ways fresher and more receptive than Easterners toward learning the pure spiritual qualities of Dharma. With their free beginner's minds, they are unrestricted by many hard and stale traditions. But in some ways, the Western freedom habit can result in restriction. People are encouraged to have freedom without pause; they don't pay attention to when or where to be free. They don't have the great view about real freedom that depends on good intention with farsightedness for the benefit of self and others. As a result, whatever they want to do, they just do it in an opportunistic frenzy, as many Asian businesspeople do, without examining until the time when something goes wrong. Then they have to repeat their action again to repair the wrong done, and having to repeat is the cause of being bound.

Sometimes the Western honesty habit is the cause of regret. People are not taught the great view about refined honesty that depends on good intention with farsightedness for the benefit of self and others. Only gross honesty is taught, without examining the effect it will have and what the result will be. When circumstances change and the previous truth becomes false, their honesty causes frustration and they must repeat the truth again with a new truth to repair the wrong done. They do not notice that inconsistency is the cause of disloyalty and instability, and that having to repair is the cause of being bound. But if I judge in an uncontrived manner, I sometimes think that my Western friends' honest, straight, blurting emotions that come from democratic tradition are much closer to the Buddha Dharma than the dishonest, bent, repressed emotions that come from the misinterpretation of religious tradition. Sometimes, through their freedom habit, Westerners depend less on hierarchical social phenomena and more on their temporary confidence in the power of the individual and each person's capacity to do what he wants to do.

Sometimes the Western freedom habit causes honesty to become blurting, and blurting habit is the cause of negative reaction from others. People who don't have the great view of refined response with farsightedness for the benefit of self and others just give crude blurting responses without examining. Then, like premature ejaculation, the timing is wrong and the target is missed, causing unintentional misinterpreting and misunderstanding. So, speed becomes delay and they must repeat the response again in order to repair the wrong done, and having to repair is the cause of being bound.

Sometimes because of previous karmic debt, unintentionally we can cause anger and misunderstandings. Some misunderstandings come not just from physical appearances but also from sound.

For example, because I never studied English in school, I never learned how to speak English in a proper way. But still, in my broken English, I can communicate about small issues, although I have difficulty making abbreviations. Once in Palm Springs, I went with a friend to a realtor's office to inquire about a house. After my trying to explain

Pointing skyward in Nepal, 1991.

to the realtor what I wanted, she said with a frown on her face, "I don't understand all your explanations. What do you actually want? Do you want to buy a condominium or a house?" Her frowning stare made me nervous, so I wanted to answer her simply by abbreviating and I said, "Either is fine, a house or a condom." Then the realtor frowned even more.

Some misunderstandings come not just from sound but from physical appearances.

For example, once before leaving the San Diego airport, I needed to go to the bathroom. At that time my hair was long, and in order to be comfortable I was wearing an Indian lungi, which is a long piece of cotton wrapped around the waist, resembling a skirt. I went into the gentlemen's room, and while I was washing my hands, two gentlemen entered. Because they thought I was a woman, immediately they left, stood next to the door, and waited for me to come out. Because they didn't want to miss their airplane, they were in a hurry. But I was not in a hurry. So they became very impatient and upset and yelled to me, "Hey, lady, your restroom is over there!"

Sometimes, if you try to make things clear, it creates more disturbance.

All-Loving Noble Banner said, "You don't know who the good practitioners are until they meet with good circumstances." Artificial pretend sublime practitioners are always lured to good circumstances and are always fooled by them. When good circumstances arise, their real inner qualities emerge and change their minds to an ordinary view, toward seeking worldly power and gain, away from pure Dharma's power. This change is symbolic of a false practitioner.

You don't know who your friends are until you meet with bad circumstances. Artificial pretend good friends are always lured to you when your circumstances are good, and you are fooled by them. When bad circumstances arise, their real inner qualities emerge, and they distance themselves and change their minds to a vulgar view, toward seeking their own comfort and gain, and away from pure loyalty's power. This change is symbolic of false friends.

Good practitioners never change when good circumstances arise, as the ocean never changes when admiring rain showers from the sky above, or when praising water flows from the earth below. Good friends never change when bad circumstances arise, as pure gold never changes when a hammer beats it from above or when a fire burns it from below.

No matter what the circumstances were, my blurting, emotionally honest Western students always surrounded me with their loyalty and devotion. Even though my friends sometimes torture me with wrathful aspects of their love like a trembling earthquake, it still is very beautiful because its essence is love. Like a young colt kicking its mother in the field, they still love each other; like a young baby kicking its mother in the womb, they still love each other.

The former pure Dharma habit of the East has nearly died like a fading lamp. The present beautiful Dharma fashion of the West has nearly vanished like a dissolving rainbow.

Some years ago, Indian religions, Zen Buddhism, and Tibetan Buddhism became fashionable in the West, and many people wore robes, recited mantras, sewed round cushions, and wore prayer beads. Many young Westerners became monks, nuns, yogis, yoginis, meditators, students, scholars, philosophers, and retreatants.

The Dharma's essential point of view is the practice of substanceless mind, but according to the worldly way, these Westerners had easy, comfortable substance habits, which are difficult to change. If you put a heavy load on a young horse, it becomes tired quickly because it is used to comfortably grazing in a large, free field. If you saddle it and put it in a smaller, more confined space than it is used to in order to subdue it, it becomes paranoid, kicking and jumping wildly like a bucking bronco in a rodeo, and tries to escape, hating the one who tries to subdue it. So these young, competitive, racehorse practitioners felt confused by the heavy load that had been put on their easy-life backs.

For many lives I drank impure phenomena wine, so in this life I am still intoxicated by paranoid fantasy hallucinations. According to my fantasy hallucination phenomena, in Dharma-fashion countries, real Dharma became power-Dharma. In Dharma centers, young women students were seduced by young serious teachers' power, and the young passion-controlled teachers were seduced by the young women students' beautiful winking eyes. Old self-aggrandizing teachers were seduced by the rich sponsors' offers to make their Dharma centers fancy, and the rich sponsors were seduced by the old teachers' elaborate fantasy traditions and the wish to be special. The teachers' retinues who were controlled by their vows, and the rich sponsors who were controlled by their democracy habits, played with power and created conflicts, trying to use pure Dharma power for ordinary power. Like the superpowers who agree on disarmament but secretly sell weapons to other countries behind each other's back, directly they agreed on harmless enlightenment Dharma for all sentient beings, but indirectly

Tormas made by Rinpoche in Brekha, Bhutan.

they agreed on creating impure substance power from the pure power of Dharma tradition. In general, in Dharma-fashion countries, unless teachers have gifted wisdom mind, it is dangerous for them and their students, since they can cause material ego, power, and pride. If the students receive initiations or teachings, in order to materialize, they list and verbalize these initiations or teachings they have received rather than keeping samaya to practice, and they turn enlightenment's path into the study of a culture's knowledge for status.

When substance power is created, there is competition, and where there is competition, there is self-seeking. Where there is self-seeking, there is ego, and where there is ego, there is confusion. These days many practitioners from many countries are competing for Dharma ego with patriotic obscurations and prestige mind. If the competition is for a great worldly citadel, then there is no problem, because without competition and patriotism, momentarily, worldly power cannot develop. But if the intention is for pure Dharma, then competition and patriotism obscure the enlightenment path and close the gate to the Pureland City.

In the West, there are many nihilist Dharma practitioners with what's-happening-figure-out mind. Many philosophers with figure-out mind but no real faith and no real compassion become Dharma practitioners to teach in universities and to gain a large salary and great respect. Many journalists with figure-out mind and nihilist ideas become Dharma practitioners to report slanderously about Dharma gossip and gain fame for their outstanding reporting. Many athletes with figure-out mind become Dharma practitioners to start yoga clubs. Many authors with figure-out mind become Dharma practitioners to get ideas for new books. Many artists with figure-out mind become Dharma practitioners to find new colors to express their new fantasies. Many entertainers with figure-out mind become Dharma practitioners to have Dharma lunches and Dharma dinners. Many Western psychologists with figure-out mind become Dharma practitioners to gain new Dharma authority to lure back their ex-patients. Many inexperienced student-mind Easterners, including me, become Dharma teachers to teach spiritually naive Westerners and make them more inexperienced about Dharma.

As soon as these people with countless figure-out intentions receive temporary results, they become retired monks, retired yogis, retired meditators, and retired retreatants. They stop sewing their round cushions and reciting their mantras, they stop respecting their teachers, and they stop praying to holy images of Buddha. Then, Dharma goes out of fashion and they become re-nihilists through apostasy.

Modern students behave very differently from ancient students of Dharma, if I judge from their histories. They are like children in a toy store who want to play with all the toys at once. Grasping, they go from one toy to another, capriciously throwing each one away when they have become tired of it or have difficulty making it work. Through changing intentions and strong divorce habit, they abandon their playthings with many different excuses. When they say, "my former teacher," this means their abandoned teacher, and since all teachers are embodiments of the same Buddha essence, this means that they have abandoned the Triple Gems and the path of enlightenment. Their Dharma is like their television: they are momentarily entertained, but when they are bored with one program, they constantly channel-change until they once again become bored. Just as they leave their worldly teachers when they find out what they want to know from them, they may leave their Buddhist teachers, even though they vowed when they took refuge in the words of the Buddha that they would never abandon the Buddha, never abandon the Dharma, never abandon the Sangha, and never abandon their teacher until they reach enlightenment. According to Buddhist tradition, the teacher is the representative of the Buddha, yet they think they can divorce tradition.

Even if they like to practice, they aren't patient enough to digest their experience because of their fast-food habit. Through digestion, they could increase many qualities, but they just want to taste superficially and don't care about essential nourishment. Instead of letting experiences come patiently and naturally, they want results to appear instantly, the same way that apples are artificially waxed and oranges are dyed for an instant ripe appearance.

Besides these people, there are a few Dharma practitioners suffering from their work, their marriages, or their lovers, who are temporarily weary of samsara and just want to feel good, but they don't want to practice, because they only want to be comforted and to feel better. As a saint once said, those who ring the bell and hold the dorje without knowing what the true meaning is are no different from a cow that makes noise as it grazes with a bell around its neck.

Finally, there are very few truly serious Dharma practitioners. Though worldly people are not pleased to see Dharma practiced in a pure way, certainly the Buddhas and Bodhisattvas are smiling. Confidence does not come from having either one or many teachers. It depends on the individual's karmic faculties. Ancient Dharma students could synthesize the teachings of many different teachers into one pure lineage wisdom essence. Each teacher had different qualities and expressed different aspects of wisdom mind. They respected each beautiful form without the conception of abandoning previous forms, like noble bees who can sip the same sweet essence nectar from different flowers—some red, some blue, some white—without harming them.

According to the Buddhist way, if we cannot synthesize, it is a great obstacle to our practice. Even if we visualize countless deities, they are all contained within one essence deity and only manifest different aspects of that one essence. In visualizing one deity, all countless deities are naturally contained within that deity. As they say, "One for all and all for one." But when it comes to visualization of deities, Westerners cannot believe this.

Garden created by Rinpoche in Kunzang Gatshal.

In this present life, if we feel a contradiction between two or more teachers, then how can we synthesize the countless different aspects of our wisdom mind? And if we cannot synthesize into one essence, we are always bound by our dualistic ordinary mind and can never be released into nondualistic wisdom mind.

In ancient times, in both the East and the West, it was very rare to hear that a teacher was betrayed by his student. If a student did betray his teacher, it became an awful story. In modern times, in both the East and the West, it is very rare to hear that a student does not betray his teacher. If a student does not betray his teacher, it becomes a beautiful story.

If necessary, ancient teachers of Dharma sometimes sent their students to other teachers to expand their students' minds and increase their spiritual qualities. Modern teachers are sometimes like wardens; instead of sending their students to other teachers, they want to keep them locked in their samaya dungeons.

Ancient teachers who taught according to the Vinaya system used vows to teach discipline and understanding. Ancient teachers who taught according to the tantric system used samaya to create pure phenomena. Modern teachers sometimes misuse their vows and samaya

Always making tea and coffee for others.

as a tool for controlling their students to benefit their ordinary power. Sometimes the students, through substance morality's form, create moral perfection's immoral ego. With their ego, they create impure self-righteous phenomena, so the students become like nocturnal animals who do not want to see the light and are only comfortable in the dark. Generally, according to true Vinaya tradition, monks are taught not to be close to women and to be celibate, but modern monks, afraid to look at young women, are happy to kiss and go hand in hand with young monks.

The worldly, rational-mind teacher does not adapt to the different aspects and abilities of disciples, because his ego logic's limited means are always rigid and never expand, since their source is obscured and shallow. The wisdom-mind teacher reflects the different aspects and abilities of disciples through the skillful means of his wisdom essence, which is always beneficial and never wasted because its source is pure and profound.

I wandered in many different nations and cities in the East and West, disliking being anywhere and liking to be everywhere. Disliking and liking places does not only come from the places themselves but depends predominantly on how individual inner mood-time and karmic energy complement outer circumstances.

New Delhi: a contradiction old and new city, like mixed vegetarians and nonvegetarians.

Calcutta: a chaotic city, like New York, turned into a degenerate beggar.

Kathmandu: a cozy, simple family city, unelaborate but containing everything, including many holy places, like a magnificent antique brocade with a modern patch.

Deity dance, with Boudhanath Stupa, Nepal, in background, 1980.

In Jorpati village, Nepal, 1986. Rinpoche taught and
practiced extensively here in the 1980s and '90s.

Manila: an embellished city, like a middle-aged woman trying to look
 young through cosmetics.

Bangkok: a city of choices, where you can go in one direction
 with pure Hinayana mentality in ancient temples, or in many
 directions with many pleasures; an ancient holy city, decorated
 like saffron flowers in a modern plastic vase.

Hong Kong: an international smuggler's destination city with tidy
 police walking in lively, noisy streets.

Geneva: a resting city, like a politician retired from government.

Zurich: a rich city, like a stingy merchant who wants to bury his profit
 for many years, as if he is going to live for many eras.

Copenhagen: an inviting city, like a small fireplace with a warm fire.

Amsterdam: a soothing city, like an intimate, loving girlfriend.

London: a splendid city, like a formerly wise but now senile aristocrat.

Paris: a regal city, like a beautiful bachelor queen.

Honolulu: a relaxed city, like an uncrowded bar where everyone is
 clean and rested.

Los Angeles: a scattered city, like a teenager's sexual curiosity.

San Francisco: a clean city, like an elegant, genteel Christian graveyard.

Santa Fe: a picturesque city, like a painter's bright, simple palette, imitating Tibet.

Boston: a sophisticated city, like London without queens and dukes and falling bridges.

New York: a no-more-nothingness city,

where gentle, quiet audiences sit in theaters listening to classical concerts;

where rough, noisy audiences sit in stadiums in pandemonium watching boxing;

where high-standard-style distinguished men walk on clean avenues with glamorous women who wear fancy dresses and whisper in gentle voices;

where low-standard-style men eat hotdogs while swaggering on dirty streets with casual women who wear blue jeans and scream in vulgar voices;

where tight-minded, conservative people walk in large, clean parks, sitting on benches reading books and newspapers, calmly smoking pipes and petting poodles;

where free-minded, eccentric people walk in small, dirty parks, selling drugs, swaying with stoned bodies, sitting on benches sipping wine from paper bags and playing songs;

where many gay men embrace, some wearing leather belts for whipping each other;

where many gay women embrace wherever there is a corner;

where the CIA pays salaries to the KGB without knowing it;

where there are clean people with dirty minds;

where there are dirty people with clean minds;

where hundreds of nihilist people reject spiritual teachings;

where hundreds of spiritual teachers reject samsara's teachings;

where poor people sleep underground on low subway platforms;

where rich people sleep aboveground in high skyscraper penthouses;

where many nonpractitioners stay for their nightclub retreat to find pleasure;

where many practitioners leave for their countryside retreat to find pleasure;

where I never met before in my whole life such a malicious friend
    to whom I gave nectar and who responded with poison;
where I never met before in my whole life such loyal friends who
    served me tirelessly without expectation;
where there are no more useless things, including garbage cans;
where there are no more useful things, including the United
    Nations.

But since everything is impermanent, the aspects of all cities will change, so it is not necessary to take their descriptions seriously.

Wandering in many cities, I met:
unscrupulous friend and trustworthy friend,
fixed pure conception friend and constantly suspicious friend,
entertainer friend and anti-superficial friend,
cold miser friend and warm kindness friend,
promiscuous friend and forever thankful friend,
boring friend and kinky friend,
dictator friend and serving-minded friend,
manipulator friend and much-concerning friend,
reporter friend and non-blurting friend,
unpredictable friend and stable friend,
confused friend and determined friend,
prestige friend and humble friend,
regal princess friend and spoiled prince friend,
citygirl-style friend and farmgirl-style friend,
hunger-smelling friend and mental halitosis friend,
waxing crescent moon smiling loyalty friend and fresh flower face
    honest friend,
landable lovable friend and punishable pure intention friend,
uncontrived enthusiasm friend and missed target friend,
irritating stubbornness friend and bliss-filling surrendering friend,
extroverted nervous-making friend and introverted comforting
    friend,
soft-furred dangerous-clawed cat friend and witch angel friend,
innocent spy friend and unintentionally seductive friend,
conceited patronizing friend and self-effacing sweetness friend,
anything-can't-say friend and anything-can-say friend,

Near Lhasa at the Yonchab Tsangpo (Great Ocean River of Offering)
during a return to Tibet in 1986 when Rinpoche quietly
and tirelessly gave many teachings to Tibetan disciples.

Dharma gossiping friend and Dharma drama friend,
Dharma curiosity friend and Dharma seriousness friend,
anonymous bloodsucking friend and anonymous generosity
    friend,
unhesitating fairy-figure friend and doe-eyed integrity friend,
saying I can do anything but doing nothing friend and never
    saying I can do anything but doing everything friend.

But since everything is impermanent, the aspects of these friends will
change, so it is not necessary to take their descriptions seriously.

The cloudless sun's rays
are a lover to the young lotus,
even though the stars don't know its light.
The stainless stream
nourishes the sage,
and his natural samadhi glows,
even though the townsmen ignore its purity.

The pureless Thinley Norbu's peculiar activities suit pure-minded
    friends,
even though the too-pure brittle-minded Dharma people judge
    him.

With my ego, I gave teachings in the Far East many times for people of many different nationalities. With my ego, I gave teachings in the
Far West for people of many different personalities.

Some animals are born with their enemy inherent within them;
they are hunted for their soft, beautiful furs.

Some birds are born with their enemy inherent within them;
they are hunted to be caged for their beautiful song.

A deer is born with his enemy inherent within him;
He is hunted for his sweet-smelling musk.

An antelope is born with his enemy inherent within him.
He is hunted for his magnificent horns.

An oyster is born with his enemy inherent within him;
he is hunted for his perfect pearl.

I was born with my ego-mind enemy inherent within me;
I am hunted by jealous people for my ego qualities.

Where there is ego, there is the enemy.
Where there is ego, there is the friend.

Where there is ego, there is the student.
Where there is ego, there is the teacher.
Where there is ego, there is samsara.
Where there is ego, there is enlightenment.

With antelope in Gokarna Park, Nepal, 1984.

With elephants in Gokarna Park, Nepal, 1987.

Because of my ego, I did not think about when uncertain death would come with panting tongue. Because of my ego, my body's hair never swayed like grass in samsara's weariness wind.

In order to attain enlightenment, I must try to purify the negative paranoia of my ego. In order to attain enlightenment, I must try to create positive paranoia for my ego. In order to create positive paranoia, I must take refuge in powerful, positive protectors. But where are these powerful, positive protectors?

Fish take refuge in water, but still they are never safe from larger fish and fishermen's hooks.

Wild animals take refuge in the jungle, but still they are never safe from wilder animals and hunters' arrows.

Tame animals take refuge in human beings, but still they are never safe from being subdued and beaten.

Lovers take refuge in each other, but still they are never safe from new lovers' interference through previous karmic eye-winking link.

Children take refuge in parents, but still they are never safe from separation through death, divorce, or uncomplementary energy.

Subjects take refuge in their king's power, but still they are never safe from his increasing ambition's power and rigid laws.

Kings take refuge in their own power, but still they are never safe from revolution and their subjects' democratic ideas.

Citizens take refuge in political freedom, but still they are never safe from capitalism's greed, poverty's possibility, and the freedom to make communist revolution.

Communists take refuge in superficial equality, but still they are never safe from unavoidable, uneven power that comes from different individual karmic results.

Anarchists take refuge in their own disorder, but still they are never safe from a new dictator's control.

Dictators take refuge in their own power, but still they are never safe from guerrillas' terror.

That is why Padmasambhava said that as much as you think the lords of samsara are noble, that much will you be lured by them. But they do not have the power to give ultimate safety from fear. If you want to be free from suffering, you should take refuge in the Triple Gems, which never lure and which can rescue you from fear always.

At Rinpoche's residence in Jorpati, Nepal, with Boudhanath Stupa in background.

O Lord Buddha,
for this long time
you have given me comfort,
but I have never acknowledged it
nor let it into my mind.
For many years the snow has fallen,
but the rigid mind has never absorbed it.
For many lifetimes my samsaric habits
have hardened like dry soil.
O Lord Buddha,
with your compassion
may you plow this soil
and shower your precious teachings upon it.

I would like to take refuge in you, Lord Buddha,
until I am the same as you,
sitting tranquilly, robed in saffron,
with your equanimity gesture,
underneath the sheltering Bodhi Tree.

I would like to take refuge in your Dharma,
which is like a soft rain of nectar,
extinguishing the flame of all my passion.

I would like to take refuge in your Sangha,
who create only virtue
and are so full of compassion
they cannot cast a wrathful eye
even upon their enemy.

These images are beautiful to my outwardly dependent and de-
pressed mind. But please, I must request that you listen to my doubt.
The waves of samsara's ocean are never-ending, and lifetime after lifetime, though I am an ascetic and abandon all desirable qualities, still
I am swept away by my karma. Now I fear that my diligent effort to
reach your place will be delayed again and again, so please, Lord Buddha, can you quickly transform my object of refuge as you did for King
Indrabodhi in Oddiyana?

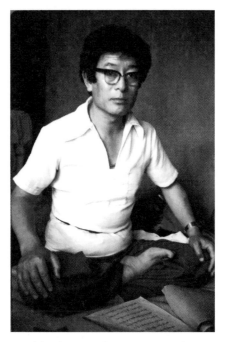

With handwritten Tibetan text, in Nepal, 1977.

Holding a deity statue of Padmasambhava in the aspect of Orgyen Dechen Gyalpo, in New York, 1990. Rinpoche designed the statue, which was made by a Nepalese sculptor.

I would like to take refuge in you, Lord Buddha,
until I am the same as you,
exalted principal deity
in the center of the wisdom light mandala,
alluringly in union with your consort
with all desirable qualities.

I would like to take refuge in your Dharma,
which can use all my passions' poison
without exception, as healing ambrosia.

I would like to take refuge in your Sangha,
who generate pure phenomena through visualization
and experience all form as wisdom deity,
All sound as wisdom mantra,
All thought as self-liberating in wisdom mind

These images are beautiful to my passion-dependent and elated mind.

But please, again, I must request that you listen. I have heard from the stories of past saints that those who cling to various visions of demons and deities are deceived; even if they sit with unbroken upward gaze, mouth hanging open, and fingernails worn down from reciting mantra, if they still do not understand the true nature of deity because their mind is tense and grasping, then deity reverses into demon, this life's blessing turns to hysteria, and in the next life they are born in the retinue of demons. O Lord Buddha, please, can you show me the true nature of deity so I can avoid this great obstacle?

Now I remember. Your messenger Vimalamitra once said that the Buddha, Dharma, and Sangha are inherent within our own uncontrived mind. So, Lord Buddha, if I take refuge in this way, will you remain in my uncontrived mind inseparably?

> I would like to take refuge in you, Lord Buddha,
> by recognizing always that
> I am the same as you,
> timelessly in clear space,
> sitting on a directionless throne of rest,
> pervading all the universe,
> youthful immortal body
> clothed in formless scarves
> of colorless light.

> I would like to take refuge in your Dharma,
> which is like a resonating song
> from the unborn sky,
> displaying existence
> as honorable teaching.

> I would like to take refuge in your Sangha,
> who have inherent self-creating spiritual qualities,
> reflecting like rainbows in crystal
> and as inseparable from the Buddha
> as rays from the sun.

In prayer before a statue of Guru Rinpoche, sculpted by Rinpoche's own hands, in Pema Osel Ling, California.

Because I believe that I will be reborn again and again until my duality mind is exhausted . . .

Because I believe that all sentient beings have been my parents since I have been reborn countless times . . .

Because I believe your teaching that we must have compassion for all sentient beings . . .

I would like to develop bodhichitta, the essence of all your teachings, which can be increased in three ways:

Like a king, with the confidence of his power, who caringly benefits his subjects. In this way, before helping others, I could first attain enlightenment for myself and then, with absolute confidence, benefit all sentient beings to attain enlightenment after me.

Like the captain of a ship who, with more caring than the king, sails with his passengers and crew until they reach the other shore together. In this way, all sentient beings and myself could attain enlightenment at the same time.

Like a shepherd who, with supreme caring, greater than the king's and the sea captain's, encourages his flock to move ahead of him and guards the safety of each one until they all reach their destination. In this way, while I myself remain in samsara's suffering, I could help all sentient beings attain enlightenment before me.

Please, may you reveal to me which of these three ways is most suitable for my faculties.

O Lord Buddha, you have taught that while increasing bodhichitta we should keep remembering four wishes for the benefit of all sentient beings. So with these wishes in my heart, I pray to you:

> May I send my daughter of love to all sentient beings as a young bride to her new husband.
> May I send my son, hero of compassion, to conquer in the raging battle of samsara.
> May I remember all sentient beings as my parents and, with no jealousy, take great joy in their good fortune, as a loving mother rejoices in her sons' success.
> May I see all sentient beings with eyes of equanimity.

> O Lord Buddha,
> may I increase bodhichitta
> with generosity
> with morality
> with patience
> with diligence
> with meditation
> with wisdom.

May the seed of my Buddha nature grow
into crops of abundance
that serve as food
to end the pitiful starvation
of all sentient beings in samsara.

O Lord Buddha,
please stay before me,
your sunrise body
on the flawless lotus cushion.
I offer all worldly existence,
including my ordinary body, speech, and mind,
to attain your non-attached
sublime body, speech, and mind.

Seated on the grounds of Kunzang Gatshal.

Because I am not the same as you,
please accept my offering
to become the same as you,
nothing-remaining space.

O Lord Buddha,
please stay before me,
your wisdom body
on the priceless jewel throne.

I offer all pure-existence qualities,
including my extraordinary
samayasattva body, speech, and mind,
to attain your jnanasattva
wisdom body, speech, and mind.

Because I am not the same as you,
please accept my offering
to become the same as you,
dustless pureland and stainless-appearance space.

O Lord Buddha,
please stay indistinguishable from me
on the egoless corpse cushion,
in your yourless body.

I offer all-encompassing existence,
including desirable qualities,
to attain the sphere of
uncreated wisdom mandala.

Because I am not different from you,
please accept this offering
to acknowledge this no-difference,
three-wisdom mandala.

*In front of the Memorial Stupa in Thimphu, constructed
under Kyabje Dudjom Rinpoche's guidance by Rinpoche
at the request of Her Majesty Ashi Phuntsho Choden of Bhutan.*

O Lord Buddha,
please stay on the indestructible,
unconditioned throne
in self-luminosity body.

I offer display of unobstructed phenomena,
including recognition of self-effulgent,
all-pervasive awareness,
to attain the already attained.

Because you and I are
the sameless same,
please accept my offering
to nothing become,
extremeless clear space.

East Bhutanese gather to receive blessings from Rinpoche,
who is scattering rice from a yellow palanquin carried through the crowd.

NAMES, TITLES, AND TERMS

Personal Names

Able Teaching of Glorious Noble Activity: Dodrup Rinpoche Thupten Thinley Palbar.

Accomplished Lord Naga: Skt. Nagarjuna (ca. 150–250); Tib. Gonpo Ludrup.

All-Knowing Loving Auspicious Majestic Accomplishment: Dilgo Khyentse Rinpoche, Tashi Paljor (1910–1991).

All-Knowing Vastly Profound Excellently Pervading: Kunkhyen Longchen Rabjam (Omniscient Longchenpa; 1308–1364).

All-Loving Display: Kunga Namrol.

All-Loving Noble Banner: Kunzang Gyaltsen.

Blood-Drinking Islander, Subduer of Evil: Thraktung Dudjom Lingpa (1835–1904). Tib. *thraktung* (Skt. heruka) means "blood-drinking," a metaphor for annihilating samsara. *Düdjom* means "subduer of evil." *Lingpa* is "Islander." In this case, "island" implies a totally different universe, extremely isolated from other lands or the material world.

Empowered Changeless True Meaning: Gyurme Ngedön Wangpo.

Enlightened Indestructible Freedom from Activity: Chatral Sangye Dorje Rinpoche (b. 1913).

Exalted Instructor of Noble Destiny: Lopön Sönam Sangpo Rinpoche.

Family Branch of Front-Facing Fortress: Dokhar Surpe Migyu.

Fearless Islander: Jigme Lingpa (1730–1798).

Fearless Wisdom Vajra: Kyabje Jigdral Yeshe Dorje Rinpoche (1904–1987).

Gently Tuned Wisdom Intelligence of Phenomena: Jamyang

Khentse Chökyi Lodrö (1893–1959), master of the nonsectarian Rime movement.

Glorious Destiny: Sönam Paldron.

Glorious Prosperous Wish: Döndrup Palmo.

Great Bliss Dharma Holder of the Vajra: Dordzin Dechen Chödzin.

Great Excellent Oddiyana: Tulku Orgyen Chechog. Also known as Tulku Orgyen Chemchog, one of the heart-sons of Khenpo Ngagchung.

Great Profound One: Longchenpa (1308–1364).

Great Scholar Victorious Speech: Khenpo Ngakchung, Ngawang Palzang (1879–1941), author of *A Guide to "The Words of My Perfect Teacher."*

Happy Long-Life Dharma: Semo Tsering Chökyi-la.

Holder of Wealth: Semo Nordzin-la.

Indestructible Great Bliss: *See* Noble Lama Indestructible Great Bliss

Indestructible Noble Glory: Se Dorje Palzang-la.

Indestructible Wisdom Teacher from Polo: Polo Khen Rinpoche Dorje (1896–1970). Also known as Polu Khen Rinpoche.

Jewel of Activity: Kyabje Thinley Norbu Rinpoche.

Jewel of Beneficial Well-Being: Phende Norbu Rinpoche.

Jewel of the Occurrence of All Qualities: Yönten Kunjung Rinpoche.

Long Life: Tsering.

Lotus of Turquoise Light: Semo Pema Yudron-la.

Melodious Long Life: Tsering Yangchen.

Noble Lama Indestructible Great Bliss: Lama Sangpo Dechen Dorje.

Noble Priestess Yogini of Phenomena Space: Shuksep Jetsunma Lochen Chönyi Zangmo (1852–1953). *Chönyi* in Sanskrit is *dharmata,* "phenomena space."

Ocean of Glorious Dharma: Lochen Chöphel Gyatso (1654–1717). Also known as Lochen Dharmashri.

Ocean of Intelligence: Lodrö Gyatso.

Peaceful God: Shantideva (eighth century).

Plaited Hair: Chang Lo.

Self-Liberated Six Senses: Shabkar Tsogdruk Rangdröl (1781–1851).

Smooth Melodious Lamp of Dharma: Sangyum Jamyang Chödrön-la.

Sole Holy Buddha Father: Padampa Sangye (d. 1117), teacher of Machik Labdrön.

Sole Mother Lamp of Labchi: Machik Labdrön (1055–1149).

Sun of Dharma: Dola Tulku Jigme Chökyi Nyima Rinpoche.
Tall Stone Emanation: Doring Tulku.
Turquoise Lamp of Firm Life: Mayum Tseten Yudron-la.
Turquoise Radiance of Great Bliss: Semo Dechen Yudron-la.
Understanding of Phenomena: Lama Lodrö Nangwa.
Victorious Great Powerful Empowerment of Speech: Shabdrung
    Ngawang Namgyal (1594–1651).
Vidyadhara of Oddiyana: Lama Orgyen Rigdzog.
Wisdom Intelligence of Phenomena: *See* Gently Tuned Wisdom
    Intelligence of Phenomena
Yellow Lama: Lama Serpo.
Younger Jewel of Conquering Speech of Dharma's Renown: Minling
    Chung Rinpoche, Ngagwang Chödrak (1908–1980).

Place Names

Above Auspicious Land: Tashigang, town in eastern Bhutan.
Accepting Mountain of Great Bliss: Len Ri Dewa Chenpo.
Auspicious Sky-Touching Castle: Tashi Nam Dzong.
Buddha's Toe-Petal Blossom Land: Nepal.
Dragonland: Bhutan.
Emerald Buddha Land: Thailand.
Forest Valley Land: Kongpo, region in southeastern Tibet.
Fruit Valley: Sikkim, known to Tibetans as Dejong ("rice valley").
Glorious Lion Great Perfection: Dzogchen Shri Singha Monastery, in
    eastern Tibet.
Golden Basin: Sershong.
Great Ocean River of Offering: Yonchab Tsangpo, the biggest river
    in Tibet and the highest major river in the world; also known as
    Yarlung Tsangpo or the Tsangpo. The river originates in western
    Tibet and passes into India.
Hidden Fern Valley: Beyul Khenpa Jong, a "hidden valley" (beyul) in
    Bhutan, sacred to Padmasambhava.
Hidden Land of Lotus Ornament: Beyul Pemakö, in southeastern
    Tibet.
Land of the Gods: Lhasa.
Lion's Castle: Seng-ge Dzong, a cave sacred to Padmasambhava,
    located to the east of Bumthang, Bhutan.

Lotus Island: Pema Ling.

Manifestation of Rejoicing: Trulga ('phrul dga').

Occurrence of All Benefits and Qualities: Yönten Kunjung.

Polu: District of the Derge region of Tibet. Also spelled Polo.

Snow Mountain Land: Tibet.

Snowland: Tibet.

Sublime Island of Ripening Liberation: Mindrolling Monastery.

Superior Great Exaltation: Dechen Teng.

Supreme Shakya Sphere: India.

Temple of Miraculous Goat-Earth Phenomena: Rasa Trulnang Tsuklakhang, in Lhasa, known as the Jokhang Temple. Lhasa ("Land of the Gods") was originally called Rasa, which meant "Land of the Goats," since goats carried the earth and stones to build the temple.

Tiger's Lair: Paro Taktsang. Also known as Tiger's Nest.

Upper Valley of Amusement: Kurtö.

Wisdom Sword Holder's Land: China.

Wish-Fulfilling Palace: Samdrup Phodrang.

Titles of Works

Accepting the Offering (dance): Tshog Len Cham.

Carriage of Omniscience: Namkhen Shingta (rnam mkhyen shing rta), a commentary by Jigme Lingpa on his *Treasury of Qualities.*

Carriage of Two Truths: Dennyi Shingta (bden gnyis shing rta), a commentary by Jigme Lingpa on his *Treasury of Qualities.*

Command of the Lion's Roar (dance): Seng-ge Dradog.

Crow Sword Dance: Pho Rog Cham.

Darkness of the Ten Directions Dispelled: Chogchu Munsel (phyogs bcu mun sel), by Longchenpa, commentary on the *Guhyagarbha Tantra.*

Entrance into Bodhisattva's Action: Skt. *Bodhicharyavatara* (The Way of the Bodhisattva); Tib. *Jangchub Sempe Chöpa La Jukpa (byang chub sems dpa'i spyod pa la 'jug pa).*

Essence of Secret Teachings: Skt. *Guhyagarbha Tantra;* Tib. *Gyu Sangwa Nyingpo (rgyud gsang ba'i snying po).*

Five Dakini Dance: Khandro De-nge Gar.

Four Heart Drops: Nyingtig Yazhi (snying thig ya bzhi), by Longchenpa.

Friend's Message: Skt. *Suhrllekha* (Letter to a Friend), by Nagarjuna; Tib. *Shetring,* short for *Shepai Tringyik (bshes pa'i spring yig).*

Ruler of the Secret Teachings' Wisdom Heart's Ornament: Sangdak Gong-gyen *(gsang bdag dgongs rgyan),* commentary on the *Guhyagarbha Tantra,* by Lochen Dharmashri.

Samantabhadra's Prayer of Basis, Path, and Result: Kuntuzangpö Shi Lam Drebu Mönlam. Also known as the Kunzang Mönlam (kun bzang smon lam), or Aspiration Prayer of Kuntuzangpo.

The Seven Treasures: Dzö Dun (mdzod bdun), by Longchenpa.

Song of the Waves of the Garuda's Wings: Khading Shoglab (mkha' lding gshog rlabs, Flight of the Garuda), by Shabkar Tsogdruk Rangdröl.

The Three Restings: Ngalso Kor Sum (ngal gso skor gsum), by Longchenpa.

Treasure of Space Phenomena: Chöying Dzö (chos dbyings mdzod, Treasury of Dharmadhatu), by Longchenpa.

Treasury of Qualities: Yönten Dzö (yon tan mdzod), also called *Treasury of Precious Qualities (Yönten Rinpoche Dzö).*

Vast Profound Heart Drop: Longchen Nyingtig (klong chen snying thig, Heart Essence of the Vast Expanse), cycle of teachings revealed by Jigme Lingpa.

Other Names and Terms

Blue Turquoise Dragon (horse): Yudruk Ngonmo.

channels and airs: Tib. tsa lung; Skt. nadi and prana.

cutting through: Tib. trekchö.

Great Gesture: Skt. Mahamudra; Tib. Chag-gya Chenpo.

Great Perfection: Tib. Dzogpa Chenpo, or Dzogchen.

Mahadeva: Tib. Lha Chen. An epithet of the Hindu god Shiva.

Mamaki (Skt. and Tib.): Wisdom Water Goddess; one of the five female Buddhas of the five Buddha families.

New School [Sarma] lineage of the Great Gesture: Sang-ngak Sarme Chag-gya Chenpo Gyupa.

Old School [Nyingma] lineage of the Great Perfection: Sang-ngak Nyingme Dzogpa Chenpo Gyupa.

samaya (Skt.; Tib. damtsig): sacred promise, vow, commitment.

simultaneous passing: Tib. thögal.

spiritual friend: Tib. chödrok.

transference into pureland: Tib. phowa.

treasure holder: Tib. tertön, treasure (terma) revealer.

Vajra Kumara (Skt.; Tib. Dorje Shonnu): Vajra Youth. Also known as Vajra Kilaya (Tib. Dorje Phurba).

Vajradhara (Skt.; Tib. Dorje Chang): Highest level of enlightenment of a Buddha according to secret mantra.

wisdom holder: Skt. vidyadhara; Tib. rigdzin.